DEATH AND HOPE
IN THE BODY OF CHRIST

DEATH AND HOPE IN THE BODY OF CHRIST

Walking With The Sheep Through The Shadows

Paul A. Reimer
Doctor of Religious Studies
BCP Retiree Coordinator

Baptist Church Planters
Grafton, Ohio

Published by Baptist Church Planters
36830 Royalton Road
Grafton, OH 44044 USA
http://www.bcpusa.org/

Copyright 2020 by Baptist Church Planters

All rights reserved. No part of this publication may be reproduced, stored in a retrieval system, or transmitted, in any form or by any means, electronic, mechanical, photocopying, recording, or otherwise, without the prior written permission of the publisher.

Printed in the United States of America on acid-free paper

Library of Congress Control Number: 2019920915

ISBN-13: 978-1-936285-06-8 (pbk)
ISBN-13: 978-1-936285-07-5 (ebk)

The press has no responsibility for the persistence or accuracy of URLs for external or third-party websites referred to in this publication and does not guarantee that any content on such websites is, or will remain, accurate or appropriate.

Cover design by Marilyn Martin

 *Dear Pastor,*

    The Apostle Paul had his Timothy, whom he led to Christ, poured his life into, and challenged as a son "to be strong in the grace that is in Christ Jesus. And the things that thou hast heard of me among many witnesses, the same commit thou to faithful men, who shall be able to teach others also."

    I've had many Pauls in my life and am thankful for all they have taught me. I dedicate this book to you, young Timothy. Officiating your very first funeral can be overwhelming, but with the Lord's help and a little direction, I'm confident you and your church can be a rich blessing to those who are grieving. In a few years, you will be able to teach other faithful men who are doing what we are doing—pointing grieving saints to the One Who is present and alive.

    May God grant you many such opportunities.

Dr. Paul

CONTENTS

Foreword	ix
Acknowledgments	xi
Introduction: What Will They Remember?	1
1. The Biblical View of Physical Death	7
2. The Arguments for a Funeral	17
3. The Patterns of Funerals	25
4. Walking with the Sheep as the Shadows Lengthen	39
5. Preparation: The Hours from Death to Good-bye	49
6. The Funeral Service: A Celebration of Life or a Preparation for Eternity?	59
7. The Graveside Service: A Necessary Parting	75
8. The Funeral Director: Co-laborer or Combatant?	83
9. The Funeral Meal: Blessing or Burden?	89
10. The Follow-Up: After the Funeral, Now What?	97
11. Your First Funeral	107
Epilogue: Hope for Today and Tomorrow	115
Resources	123
Notes	139
Bibliography	149

FOREWORD

It is not *if* you will face this; it is definitely *when*. You or someone you know will experience a death in the family. Think of it! Every family in your neighborhood, workplace, and local church is going to be affected by death. Every family! There is no event in life any more significant or painful than the death of a loved one. Hearts are broken. Sorrow is crushing. Bewilderment and questions like "How am I going to continue on?" are overwhelming.

What tremendous opportunities come to the Lord's servants to reach out and minister to those who are going through such significant sorrow. Very few situations in life provide such opportunities to serve people. In this book, Dr. Paul Reimer challenges and encourages pastors not to miss these opportunities but rather to make the most of them.

At the death of their brother Lazarus, Christ ministered to sorrowing Mary and Martha in John 11. His ministry was *personal*; He came to them. It was *practical*; He quietly and tenderly led them through reasoning that was faulty, caused by their deep sorrow. He helped them through the what-ifs. His ministry was *powerful*; it was life-giving. While we will not have the opportunity to raise people from the dead, in a very real sense, we do indeed have the opportunity to share how people can have life-changing eternal life.

I am so glad that my personal friend Dr. Reimer so capably presents vitally important considerations when helping people in this, the deepest experience of life. From ladies and food prep to funeral directors and arrangements to pastors ministering to friends who will visit, Dr. Reimer explains how to assist the family and others who want to serve the grieving. Everyone involved must serve Christ biblically and capably in meeting the needs of those who are sorrowing.

From more than forty years of ministry experience, Pastor Reimer shares with us from the heart of a pastor-shepherd. His tender, gentle spirit and loving heart show through the words and pages of this book.

He provides insights into helping us better minister to people in a way that is personal, practical, and powerful. What a great opportunity and responsibility to step into the lives of people at this most opportune moment to meet them in their greatest need.

The things of which Dr. Reimer writes are not merely words or empty theory. I know that he lives out the things of which he writes. I've experienced his sweet and comforting ministry in my own personal life. Thank you, Dr. Paul, for your time and investment in our lives, in the lives of those who will serve other grieving families, and in the lives of those to whom we will minister.

Dr. Michael Peck

ACKNOWLEDGMENTS

Funerals and memorial services can be very public, and some very private. Regardless of whether a family invites me to be a part of it or to officiate the whole, I am humbled by the opportunity. I want to thank those families who have allowed me into their lives for those hours we spent together, whether in their homes or at the funeral home, the church, or the cemetery. Much of what is recorded in this book is the fruit of those days. Dear loved ones, thank you.

Nearly twenty years ago, the Lord brought into my life Dr. Michael and Karen Peck. Their love for Christ, each other, and their flocks has made a deep impression upon me. I am honored to call Dr. Mike my friend, and we have shared many hours serving the Lord together from our distant locations. Dr. Mike was very kind to read each of my chapters and to share his wisdom and words of encouragement. Dear friend, thank you!

Ginny Sebok is the executive administrative assistant of Baptist Church Planters. Her skill in editing and her gentle questions pushed me to be concise and clarify each paragraph of this text. She willingly invested in this work, and you and I are the benefactors of her ability. Thank you, Ginny, for the hours and heart you invested in this project.

The professors of Trinity Theological Seminary of Newburgh, Indiana, are greatly trained servants of God, and I have gained much from their insight into the Word of God. However, there is one, Dr. Johnathan Pritchett, who was my advisor for the completion of my doctorate and this book, whose ability to stretch my thinking theologically has borne fruit throughout my ministry. I also remember at one point when I was ready to give up writing altogether that he simply asked me to pursue an area that I had not considered. It helped me to get back to the Book and the books and thus finish this book. Thank you, Dr. Pritchett, for your investment in my life.

Pastor Richard N. Pettitt was old enough to be my father but physically strong enough to beat me in every sport in which we competed:

golf, tennis, and especially baseball. Pastor Pettitt was also my mentor, my pastor, and, for ten years, my boss. His knowledge of the Word, his skill in ministry, and his love for people were shared with me and observed by me. He didn't try to clone me to be another Pastor Pettitt, but, understanding my gifts and my shortcomings, he challenged me to be all God wanted me to be. I would agree with him that the ten years we served side by side were some of the greatest years of our public ministries. Thank you, Pastor Pettitt, for believing in me and investing your life in me.

The Lord has brought dozens of missionary couples into my life. I am grateful for their insight and sharing of the experiences and observations of their adopted countries. Thank you, fellow laborers in the Gospel, for sharing your stories with me.

Solomon wrote that there is no end to the writing of books. That's true; however, I am thankful for every author who has taken the time to address the needs of people and, by doing so, has ministered to those who are dying and the loved ones left behind who grieve. Thank you for taking the time to share your expertise for me and others to read and learn.

To President Steve Little and Vice President David Whipple, administrators of Baptist Church Planters, who not only encouraged me by offering the mission's resources but also offered to publish this book with the view of helping young and/or inexperienced missionaries and pastors to be better ministers to their flocks, thank you!

I would like to express my appreciation as well to Holly Monteith for her copy editing skills and to Marilyn Martin of Register Graphics for her cover design. Their skills, recommendations, and tenacious efforts in preparing this book for publication have made it a joy to work with them.

My first pastor's wife, Mrs. Evelyn Weaver, told me while I was studying for the ministry about the importance and the indispensability of the pastor's wife. She was so right, and God in His mercy and grace gave me the best. Debbie and I began serving the Lord together before we were married, and she has been at my side for more than forty-five years of ministry. Thank you, Debbie, for all the hours you spent alone while I read and wrote. Thank you for spending lonely hours on our favorite beach while I pored over other men's and women's writings. Thank you for reading to me while we traveled, and especially for encouraging me to complete what I had started. I could not have finished this without you. You have been God's gift to me for life and ministry.

And thank You, dear Lord, for putting the idea of this book into my head in the first place. Thank You for the privilege of serving You and ministering to grieving families. Thank You for the strength and time to complete this project. May You use it to train and build up young men and women to better minister to those who are walking through the shadows of life. I am forever grateful for Your presence in my life and for the blessed hope that stirs me every time I stand before those who weep. Thank You, my Lord and Savior.

INTRODUCTION
What Will They Remember?

How many funerals have you attended where an hour after the service, you could not remember a word the preacher said? Did you just go through the traditional and expected ritual, shed a few tears, reminisce over a few events, have a Thanksgiving-like meal, exchange hugs with people you had never met before that day, drive home, and return to your normal life?

Funerals are emotionally charged events—exhausting in and of themselves. But most often before the service, there has already been a whirlwind of activity—meetings, decisions, phone calls, housing arrangements, meals planned and prepared—again, exhausting. You should not be surprised that the bereaved cannot remember a thing you said or did. So, do you just get them through this societal expectation and move on, or do you expect them to remember each salient point you make?

I have concluded that there are two essential truths, two powerful thoughts, that I want the mourners to remember and draw from in the days ahead.[1] These two thoughts can and ought to be communicated through your initial contact with the family and into the days and weeks to follow. You communicate them by your words, your presence, and your demeanor. These two points are found in the event that is as close to our contemporary funeral and memorial services as I have found in the Scriptures.

Let me take you to that event, which occurred in a little village named Bethany in first-century Israel. You will remember it well. You have gone there many times already. In many ways, it should mirror the last memorial service you attended. You will find it in John 11:1-45.

In this event, two sisters faced the sickness and eventual death of their dear brother. These three siblings were not simply faces in the crowd to our Savior. They were dear friends, and He loved them. Surely when faced with illness and dying, they could expect the Savior to intercede—but He did not!

> Now a certain *man* was sick, *named* Lazarus, of Bethany, the town of Mary and her sister Martha. . . . Therefore his sisters sent unto him, saying, Lord, behold, he whom thou lovest is sick. When Jesus heard *that*, he said, This sickness is not unto death, but for the glory of God, that the Son of God might be glorified thereby. Now Jesus loved Martha, and her sister, and Lazarus. When he had heard therefore that he was sick, he abode two days still in the same place where he was. Then after that saith he to *his* disciples, Let us go into Judaea again.
>
> . . . Our friend Lazarus sleepeth; but I go, that I may awake him out of sleep. Then said his disciples, Lord, if he sleep, he shall do well. Howbeit Jesus spake of his death: but they thought that he had spoken of taking of rest in sleep. Then said Jesus unto them plainly, Lazarus is dead. And I am glad for your sakes that I was not there, to the intent ye may believe; nevertheless let us go unto him. Then said Thomas, which is called Didymus, unto his fellow disciples, Let us also go, that we may die with him. Then when Jesus came, he found that he had *lain* in the grave four days already.[2]

Very soon you will have your first funeral, and I want you to look at it in light of this somber occasion. Keep in mind that if Jesus, the Son of God, can do nothing about death, then anything He said or did would amount to nothing! If the Son of God cannot defeat the last enemy, then whatever else He did would be only temporal. If the Son of God is not victorious over the King of Terrors,[3] then He is not the Lord of lords, nor the King of kings, nor the Son of God!

The Son of God—Death and Dying

There are some things we understand about death and dying. Because we're related to Adam, we will all face death. "For as in Adam all die" (1 Cor. 15:22a). There are many ways to die, and death can come at any time. Whether in the womb or a hundred years later, death comes knocking. We know these things, but we struggle when death knocks at our door! In John 11:3, it is stated clearly that the sisters believed Jesus loved and had a very deep and personal affection for their brother. Surely as soon as Jesus became aware of His friend's illness, He would *do* something about it!

We do not struggle with the physical or even the doctrinal reasons for illness and death—those we understand. We struggle with how a loving and powerful God would allow it to happen. Even more than that, how could this loving and powerful God, having been informed, allow His friend to die? "When he had heard therefore that he was sick, he abode two days still in the same place where he was" (John 11:6).

Was Jesus being callous toward His friends, or was He powerless? No, neither! He had at least three reasons not to hurry. First, the day Jesus heard about it, Lazarus was already dead! Jesus said, "Our friend Lazarus sleepeth" (John 11:11).[4] Consider this well. Jesus heard about His friend while He was near the place where John the Baptist ministered. Bethany is at least a two-day walk. Jesus then waited two days after He heard of Lazarus' illness. When He did arrive, Mary told Him Lazarus had been dead four days.[5] So when Jesus heard the news, Lazarus was already dead! No need to hurry. Second, Jesus has the power over death *and* the grave. He is the omnipotent God—no need to hurry. Third, since Jesus has this authority over life and death, there must be something else here that His friends need to know. Therefore, there is the need *not* to hurry.

The Son of God—Death and Doubt

During the days following Lazarus' death, we see grief and tears, confidence and doubts. Similarly, when death knocks at our doors, some will deny it, some will smile through tears, some will be overwhelmed with grief, and some will seem stoic. Some will wade their way through a sea of memories of the past, and others will be overcome with fears regarding the future. Some will be filled with unshakable confidence, and others will be filled with doubts. The first one we meet during these days of grief is a sister, Martha.

> Now Bethany was nigh unto Jerusalem, about fifteen furlongs off: And many of the Jews came to Martha and Mary, to comfort them concerning their brother. Then Martha, as soon as she heard that Jesus was coming, went and met him: but Mary sat *still* in the house. Then said Martha unto Jesus, Lord, if thou hadst been here, my brother had not died. But I know, that even now, whatsoever thou wilt ask of God, God will give *it* thee.[6]

Her words were filled with faith and hope—faith that God would hear the prayers of His Son and hope that He would pray now. Martha believed in the healing power of Jesus and His influence with his Father.

Rather than pray, Jesus chose to bring her one more step in her faith, and she confessed three truths.

> Jesus saith unto her, Thy brother shall rise again. Martha saith unto him, I know that he shall rise again in the resurrection at the last day. Jesus said unto her, I am the resurrection, and the life: he that believeth in me, though he were dead, yet shall he live: And whosoever liveth and believeth in me shall never die. Believest thou this? She saith unto him, Yea, Lord: I believe that thou art the Christ, the Son of God, which should come into the world.[7]

Martha declared her belief in Jesus' power to raise the dead. She believed He is the Christ, the Son of God. She also believed He is God incarnate. Jesus challenged her faith, and she stood firm so that even in the face of death, she had no doubt. Next, we meet Martha's sister Mary.

> The Jews then which were with her in the house, and comforted her, when they saw Mary, that she rose up hastily and went out, followed her, saying, She goeth unto the grave to weep there. Then when Mary was come where Jesus was, and saw him, she fell down at his feet, saying unto him, Lord, if thou hadst been here, my brother had not died.[8]

Mary also believed Jesus to be the Christ, but she was disappointed that He had not come earlier. There will always be those disappointments when someone dies—it was too soon; she was too young; he was needed so much. But then there were those on that day who were filled with doubts. "And some of them said, Could not this man, which opened the eyes of the blind, have caused that even this man should not have died?" (John 11:37).

How will those to whom you minister face the deaths of their loved ones? How will they face their own? Will it be with an unshakeable faith, disappointment, or soul-shattering unbelief? If not for what Jesus says and does next, life and death would be frightening, even terrifying.

The Son of God—Death Defeated

Jesus had made it very clear that the gates of hell[9] cannot prevail against Him; death cannot hold Him or deter Him. He is the Resurrection and the Life! If He is not the Son of God Who can and does defeat death, then everything said by Him and about Him is a lie.

> Jesus therefore again groaning in himself cometh to the grave. It was a cave, and a stone lay upon it. Jesus said, Take ye away the stone. Martha, the sister of him that was dead, saith unto him, Lord, by this time he stinketh: for he hath been *dead* four days. Jesus saith unto her, Said I not unto thee, that, if thou wouldest believe, thou shouldest see the glory of God? Then they took away the stone *from the place* where the dead was laid. And Jesus lifted up *his* eyes, and said, Father, I thank thee that thou hast heard me. And I knew that thou hearest me always: but because of the people which stand by I said *it*, that they may believe that thou hast sent me. And when he thus had spoken, he cried with a loud voice, Lazarus, come forth. And he that was dead came forth, bound hand and foot with graveclothes: and his face was bound about with a napkin. Jesus saith unto them, Loose him, and let him go.[10]

Here is the climax of the memorial service—the one Martha and Mary believed could happen, if only Jesus willed it to be so. In response to Christ's command, the dead man was raised from the grave and restored to his family! Hallelujah!

When a family in your congregation comes face-to-face with death, two questions need to be answered—every time! The first is this: "Where is God?" That was the question on both Martha's and Mary's lips. "Where were you?" The second question is this: "Does death end it all? Is death the final victor, and is everything I believe only for the here and now—just a temporary balm to get me through the tough times of life?"

From the moment you learn of the dying and death of someone's loved one, and in the days that follow, it is your opportunity, your privilege, your duty, to answer those two questions with two essential and powerful truths. Whatever else you can do for the family and friends is wonderful, but they need to know in no uncertain terms that "God is here, and He will never leave you" and that "death does not have the final victory for Jesus Christ is the Resurrection and the Life. The bands of death could not hold Him, and they will not hold your loved one either."[11]

In the following chapters, we will pursue principles and practical steps you can take to communicate these essential and power truths by pointing those who are overwhelmed with grief toward the living God Who is here. You will learn what you can do before, during, and after the funeral to help those whom you love and to whom you minister. You will find instruction, ideas, and resources you can use to care for those in your church and others in your community.

Who am I to write such a book? I learned from the best: Pastor Richard N. Pettitt. He ministered as a "dying man to dying men"[12] for sixty years throughout the United States, the Caribbean, and Africa. I always marveled at how he and Mrs. Pettitt ministered to the loved ones in our church at First Baptist of Findlay, Ohio. Whether the result of illness or accident, whether a teenager or a young mother to be, whether a family man or a dear old saint ready to go Home, Pastor Pettitt taught me by example and principle how to minister to the flock going through the valley of the shadow of death. The Lord has also given my wife, Debbie, and me the privilege to minister in Altoona, Iowa, as lay workers; in Findlay as an assistant pastor; and in Newark, Ohio, as pastor. For nearly fifty years, we have had the awesome privilege of caring for so many people: those who were dying and the families they left behind. I also have "officiated" and participated in many funerals—those of family members, members of our churches, friends, and total strangers.

It has been my hope and prayer that before a brother is asked to "officiate" my funeral, I would be able to communicate to you, young Timothy, how you, too, can "Walk with the Sheep through the Shadows."

CHAPTER ONE

THE BIBLICAL VIEW OF PHYSICAL DEATH

Louis Berkoff wrote, "There is the sense, the fear, that physical death is not natural, but an unnatural separation of that which belongs together."[1] Falling in love, marriage, birth, and growing up—these are as natural as breathing in and out. But death? Death appears to be so out of order with the rest of God's creative acts. What part does death play in the human experience? We begin with the origin of the human body.

The Origin of the Human Body

God created man on the sixth day.[2] God formed man, squeezing him into shape out of the dust of the ground.[3] When man was completely formed, God breathed into his nostrils the breath of life, and man became a living soul. God gave man everything he needed for life: a place to dwell, food to eat, and a reason to live. Every living creature follows this pattern—beginning life, consuming what is needed to sustain life, and fulfilling the purpose for life.

God created the beasts and man on the same day. However, though there is no commentary regarding the creation of beasts, God made it clear that the nature of man was significantly different. Created in the image of God, bearing intellect and volition, man was given verbal responsibilities and boundaries. Under this economy, man became obligated to his Creator.

David marveled in his very soul at the work of the Creator. "I will praise thee; for I am fearfully *and* wonderfully made: marvelous *are* thy works; and *that* my soul knoweth right well."[4] Everything about this body was designed to grow, sustain, protect, and reproduce life. In God's reflection on man's disobedience to His directions and subsequent consequences, we learn that the original design of this body was to live forever.

> And the LORD God said, Behold, the man is become as one of us, to know good and evil: and now, lest he put forth his hand, and take also of the tree of life, and eat, and live for ever: Therefore the LORD God sent him forth from the garden of Eden, to till the ground from whence he was taken.[5]

Through the provision of the Tree of Life in the Garden, the man and his wife could have lived forever, enjoying the gifts and presence of their Creator God, but there was in this Paradise a major paradigm shift.

The Degrading of Human Flesh

Through a single act of man, this very good and perfect creation of God became degraded, and death was the result. "And unto Adam he said, Because thou has hearkened unto the voice of thy wife and hast eaten of the tree, of which I commanded thee, saying, Thou shalt not eat of it"; the ground was cursed, sorrow and thorns filled their lives, and at the end of life, they returned to the ground, "for out of it wast thou taken: for dust thou art, and unto dust shalt thou return."[6] Immediately upon the man's disobedience, Adam died spiritually. This meant his spiritual state was degraded, and the enmity between God and man was established. Spiritual death is passed in Adam's race from one generation to the next, "for as in Adam all die" (1 Cor. 15:22).[7] Though spiritual death took place immediately, it would not be for nearly a millennium that illness, disease, and physical death would finally have victory. "And all the days that Adam lived were nine hundred and thirty years: and he died."[8] Physical death is the inevitable result of Adam's sin, not only for himself but for all of his natural descendants (Rom. 5:12, 14).[9] This of course was not true for Jesus, for His physical being is the fruit of the seed of the woman and the work of the Holy Spirit resulting in the virgin birth and bypassing the Adamic nature; thus He had no sin nature.[10] The foundation of the hope you will communicate during the funeral will be that this One who knew no sin became sin for all mankind so that He could become the substitutionary sacrifice to die in their stead. This He did by dying in their place.[11]

As you read the rest of the Genesis genealogy in chapter 5, you come face-to-face with the reality that "in Adam all die." It was not how man was created; it is, in fact, unnatural. This was a major paradigm shift, and man has had to adjust. Fast-forward to the twenty-first century, and man is still adjusting. Doctors, pharmacies, hospitals, extended-care facilities, funeral homes—all of these institutions, educators, scientists, tech companies, and more are dealing with the "unnatural" fact of dying and death. In 2016, in America alone, we spent $3.3 trillion on health care.[12] Average funeral costs in America have risen 28.6 percent, from $5,582 in 2004 to $7,181 in 2014.[13] Dying and death are big business in our country, and it affects everyone. Dying and death are facts of life, but death is and will continue to be so unnatural!

There is coming a time, because of the death, burial, and resurrection of Christ, that there will no longer be a need for all of these services. As it says in Revelation 21:4, "And God shall wipe away all tears from their eyes; and there shall be no more death, neither sorrow, nor crying, neither shall there be any more pain: for the former things are passed away." But for now, you are needed to walk with the sheep through this dark valley, to help them face their enemy, Death, and to introduce them to the One Who can give them hope.

Death, the Enemy

"The last enemy that shall be destroyed is death."[14] Of all the hostiles, of all the adversaries man faces, the "last enemy," the final one, is Death.[15] When my son was quite young, he loved playing the video game *Super Mario Bros*. It is designed to test the increasing skills of the player through thirty-two levels. At each level are obstacles that will either set you back or "kill" you. By the time you reach the thirty-second level (eight worlds with four levels each), you must have collected enough tools and developed enough skills to be able to defeat the final enemy, Bowser. I remember the day my son told me with a sense of satisfaction and joy that he had defeated the "last enemy." The problem with the game is that after the last enemy is vanquished, the game is over; however, for the believer, because the last enemy has been defeated, so much more is to come!

The work of Christ on the cross and his resurrection bring the message of hope to the grieving family. Death has been destroyed! Consider the apostle's argument. He begins by clearly stating the Gospel that he proclaimed. "For I delivered unto you first of all that which I also received, how that Christ died for our sins according to the scriptures; And that he was buried, and that he rose again the third day according to the scriptures" (1 Cor. 15:3-4).

I have been disappointed many times at the funerals I have attended that this crowning truth, this fundamental of the faith, is never even mentioned—not even in passing![16] My dear Timothy, if there is no resurrection, if Christ is not raised from the dead, then you have no message of hope.

The Old Testament View of Death

In the Old Testament, we read of "natural" and violent deaths. The first one recorded for us was a murder.[17] There is no record of a funeral, a time of mourning, only the attempt of the guilty brother to hide his sin. It would seem that Abel's body was simply left in the field where it lay. From the Genesis genealogy in chapter 5 to the end of the book, chapter 50, there are the records of thirty-one individual deaths besides all those who died during the flood. As to the response and/or ritual associated with them, it develops as time passes.

In Genesis 23, Abraham mourned and wept for Sarah, his wife. The words are descriptive. To "mourn" and to "weep" mean that Abraham tore at his hair, beat his chest, wailed, and lamented in his grief.[18] After rising from either a prone or kneeling position, Abraham addressed the children of Heth, in whose land he was and whose name, incidentally, means "terror"![19] He requested from them a place to bury Sarah "out of his sight." Out of respect for him, they offered him the freedom to choose any place. A transaction ensued between Abraham and Ephron—a cave and the surrounding land were purchased for four hundred shekels. Since this is the first mention of shekels, it is difficult to place a value on a shekel, but at the time, it appears the merchants used it as a measure of weight, not as a stamped coin.[20] This was the first property owned by the people of Israel, and it is still a sacred site four thousand years later.

At age 175, Abraham died. "Then Abraham gave up the ghost, and died in a good old age, an old man, and full *of years*; and was gathered to his people" (Gen. 25:8). The phrase "gathered to his people" is literal in two ways. First, in Luke 16, we read of Abraham's bosom and the appearance of other believers with him. Second, Abraham's body is laid in the same tomb as Sarah's, and others followed. By the end of Genesis, Sarah, Abraham, Isaac, Rebekah, and Leah were buried in the cave and field purchased from Machpelah, which is now called Hebron.[21] Over the years of my ministry, it has been just as common for family members to be buried in the same cemetery—grandparents, parents, and children. For that family, it becomes sacred ground.

When Jacob died (Gen. 49:33), Joseph commanded the Egyptian ritual of mourning to take place.[22] First, the body was embalmed with spices, and seventy days of mourning followed. With Pharaoh's permission, Jacob's family then carried the body back to Canaan to bury him in Machpelah with his fathers. After seven days of mourning were concluded, they returned to Egypt, and there the family feud was buried with confessions and forgiveness. The last death we read of in Genesis is Joseph's. He is embalmed and entombed with the promise that when Israel returns to Canaan, his bones will go with them. In life and death, family was important.

For the most part, the Old Testament writer's conclusion regarding death was to view it as life's end, a terrible loss. The hope was to die when you were "full of years" and that death would be quick and merciful.[23] However, there is more to the Old Testament theology than death as the end of existence. Man is material and immaterial; he has a body, soul, and spirit. When the body dies, the soul separates from it (Ps. 90:10).[24]

As to the future of the body and soul of man, at least two views are communicated. A limited number of references are made to a type of soul sleep. In Psalm 6:5, we read, "For in death *there is* no remembrance of thee: in the grave who shall give thee thanks? God is worthy of praise, and the grave is silent" (Ps. 88:11). However, we also read of David's confidence in a future blessing. After the walk through the valley of the shadow of death, the psalmist cries, "Surely goodness and mercy shall follow me all the days of my life: and I will dwell in the house of the LORD for ever" (Ps. 23:6). Then there is the testimony of Job, who experienced more than most fathers could even imagine with the tragic death of his ten children and his personal physical suffering. "And *though* after my skin *worms* destroy this *body*, yet in my flesh shall I see God: Whom I shall see for myself, and mine eyes shall behold, and not another; *though* my reins be consumed within me" (Job 19:26-27). Somewhere in Job's theological training, he had come to believe in a bodily resurrection. But what happens between a man's death and his resurrection from the dead?

Though recorded in the New Testament, we clearly witness the immediate destiny of the righteous and wicked dead in the Old Testament economy through the account of the rich man and Lazarus.[25]

> There was a certain rich man, which was clothed in purple and fine linen, and fared sumptuously every day: And there was a certain beggar named Lazarus, which was laid at his gate, full

of sores, And desiring to be fed with the crumbs which fell
from the rich man's table: moreover the dogs came and licked
his sores. And it came to pass, that the beggar died, and was
carried by the angels into Abraham's bosom: the rich man also
died, and was buried; And in hell he lift up his eyes, being
in torments, and seeth Abraham afar off, and Lazarus in his
bosom. (Luke 16:19-23)

Their flesh was buried, but we see the reality of the immaterial part of the deceased men before the resurrection. The rich man was in torment and was begging for relief. Lazarus was with Abraham, and in contrast to his earthly life, he was experiencing the comforts afforded the righteous. As we will see, there are similarities with the dead no matter which side of the resurrection of Christ.

Jesus' Response to Death

Jesus, the Man of Sorrows, was acquainted with our grief. His earthly life began and ended around death. In an attempt to end God's plan before it began, King Herod ordered the death of infants and toddlers in the birthplace of our Savior. At the end of His earthly ministry, another ruler, Pontius Pilate, in an effort to keep peace in Judea, ordered the death of Jesus. Through God the Father's intervention of an escape to Egypt and the resurrection of our Savior, Jesus' claim was fulfilled. "The gates of hell" could not, cannot, overpower the plan and purpose of God.

As you watch our Savior throughout his earthly journey, you will note with joy and hope that the enemy, Death, submitted to Him every time. The son of the widow of Nain was raised to life on his way to the cemetery (Luke 7:11-15). Jairus' daughter was brought to life while she "slept" on her bed (Luke 8:41-55). Also, as we have already noted, His friend, Lazarus, after all hope was gone and he was sealed in a tomb, immediately responded to the omnipotent Christ. "Lazarus, come forth!" (John 11). The gates must open when "the Resurrection and the Life" calls your name. "Believest thou this?"

The New Testament View of Death

As we move into the age of the New Testament, it is this major event that cements the hopes of the Old Testament, emboldens the disciples of Christ, and brings believers comfort in the midst of their sorrows—the resurrection of our Savior, Jesus Christ. The Lord had taught His disciples well during His earthly ministry, but now His Holy Spirit enlightened them even more regarding so many truths, including death.[26]

> And as they spake unto the people, the priests, and the captain of the temple, and the Sadducees, came upon them, Being grieved that they taught the people, and preached through Jesus the resurrection from the dead. (Acts 4:1-2)

The reality of life after death, the resurrection of the body, and the eternal fellowship with the Son are in every message of these early preachers. The Sadducees categorically rejected any bodily resurrection, and to have this "disturbing" truth connected with Jesus pained them to no end.[27] They must put an end to this "new" teaching. The attempts to silence them included threats, beatings, imprisonment, and martyrdom. Years would pass, and the message of the resurrected Christ and His vicarious blood atonement on behalf of mankind would remain in their crosshairs until one of their "heroes turned enemy" stood before them.[28] Their determination to stop the message would, in effect, send Paul all the way to Rome preaching Jesus Christ crucified and risen.

Martyrdom would eventually silence the messenger, but not the message. The Gospel of Christ would be proclaimed by others. Messenger after messenger would face a similar fate, but the message lives on. Tertullian in his second-century writing *Apologeticus* observes the power of the Gospel. It is just as true now as it was then: "The blood of the martyrs is the seed of the Church."[29]

Was it simply an idea that lived on, a notion adopted and adapted by the New Testament saints? They surely understood that death was the just judgment of God upon sinful man.[30] They were acquainted with death through injury, disease, violence, and martyrdom; however, Paul's view of death was the prevailing outlook on the eventuality.

> But none of these things move me, neither count I my life dear unto myself, so that I might finish my course with joy, and the ministry, which I have received of the Lord Jesus, to testify the gospel of the grace of God. (Acts 20:24)

The apostle lays out the hope of the believer facing death in his dissertation on the resurrection. The Corinthians had many gifted teachers, but they were deficient in that doctrine which gives the grieving hope.

The Church Grieves with Hope

Jesus faced His own death with apprehension and agony, yet with acceptance (Matt. 26:39). His death was the substitutionary atonement for sin.[31] His resurrection is the proof that His death satisfied the holiness and justice of God for all mankind.[32] It was because of the finished work on the cross that the writer of Hebrews echoed what Jesus declared from the cross: it is finished; the work of redemption has paid in full our debt, and now we can look beyond the grave with hope!

> Looking unto Jesus the author and finisher of *our* faith; who for the joy that was set before him endured the cross, despising the shame, and is set down at the right hand of the throne of God. (Heb. 12:2)

In 1 Corinthians 15, the apostle plays with the possibilities of *if* Jesus had not risen from the dead. To the Christian, the idea is unthinkable. He is alive—the tomb is empty, the five hundred plus witnesses attest to this fact.[33] But I have been a witness at too many funerals where no mention of the living Christ was made. If the resurrection of Christ is lost at the funerals we officiate, then

- our preaching is in vain (verse 13),
- our faith is in vain (verse 13),
- we are false witnesses (verse 15),
- we are still in our sins (verse 17),
- the dead in Christ are forever dead (verse 18), and
- we who are still alive are of all men to be pitied (verse 19).

Thank God this is not the case, for "He is risen!" This fact, along with the truth that our sins have been paid for through the blood of Christ, changes the message and the whole atmosphere during the memorial service. There is hope!

- Christ is the firstfruits, the beginning of the resurrection of the dead (verse 20).
- In Adam, we all die, but in Christ we shall be resurrected (verse 22).
- In the resurrected and ascended Christ resides all authority in heaven and earth. He has put all enemies under His feet, and the last enemy, Death, shall be destroyed (verses 24–25).

- It gives purpose to the suffering and persecution experienced by Paul and all other believers (verses 30–32).
- It is the power that transforms this terrestrial body into that which can live forever, a celestial body; that is, the body in its current state cannot inherit eternity—it must be changed (verses 40–44, 48–50).

Even armed with this knowledge, there will be mourning at the death of a loved one. Paul speaks of the sorrow at the death of a Christian by the surviving saints.[34] This sorrow can be intense, but it can be mitigated by the presence of the resurrected Christ. In sorrow can be hope—a calm and solid assurance regarding the future.

You will be tempted to dance around death by spending much time on memorializing the one departed. You will offer words of solace by speaking of that beloved father or grandfather being in the presence of God in a place called heaven. Memorializing the departed and comforting the sorrowing can and must be done. But remember, without the resurrected Christ, the One Who has defeated the final enemy, there is no foundation for hope. Make much of the One Who died and rose again, and you will offer hope in sorrow and the presence of the living Christ in the pain of the moment.

 CHAPTER TWO

THE ARGUMENTS FOR A FUNERAL

With the average cost of funeral home services rising "faster than virtually everything else over the last thirty years,"[1] among other reasons, many Americans are questioning the traditional funeral. We will consider the changing patterns in funerals in the next chapter, but first, let us answer this: Is there any value in a funeral regardless of what is or is not included? I am not trying to be insensitive in considering this, rather, quite the contrary. The majority of people die in an institution. Eighty percent of Americans would opt to die at home, but the truth is that only 20 percent do. Sixty percent die in acute-care hospitals and 20 percent in nursing homes.[2] So why not just let the institutions decide the best way to dispose of the body and allow the insurance to cover the costs?

Just writing that last sentence caused me to withdraw in pain. Could you, as a family member or a close friend, turn this responsibility over to a corporation that will contract for the most economical method that will give the greatest return on the dollar? It would seem to be the most cost-effective, and we could get back to living—or could we? More and more people are paying funeral homes to care for their pets that have died. They have been "a part of the family" for years, even decades. It comes across as heartless to think we can set out their remains at the curb for waste management to collect. Likewise, in the minds of most people, it is right and proper to take care how we handle our loved ones' last stage of life.

The obvious value is that a funeral provides the opportunity for the family to be involved in directing the care for the body and honoring the one whom they have loved and cared for. The loss of a loved one affects the entire being—body, soul, and spirit. The effects reach into the social, economic, and emotional lives of your parishioners. Many find it difficult, if not impossible, to carry on their normal activities. What about the friends of the departed and those of the survivors? They are struggling, too. They miss their friend and hurt for the survivors. When the family members are part of a local church, the believers are commanded to weep with those who weep.[3] The funeral is a wonderful opportunity to come alongside to minister to the friends who have suffered loss. The funeral service, along with the activities before and after, is not an end in itself. These traditional, if not ritual, acts provide an opening to honor the deceased and begin to deal with the loss.

The Nature of Loss

You will remember that death is unnatural. Death is the enemy. It is also something God hates.[4] It is this unnatural enemy that charges into all our lives and robs us of what we love with all our hearts—people. Death can take months, even years, through disease or in an unexpected moment. The one whom others would give their lives for is stopped on a busy highway to make a lefthand turn, and a distracted driver plunders the family of a precious wife and mother. Every promise made, every dream ever shared, is instantly, irrevocably, gone. The loss is overwhelming.

In addition to the physical loss of a best friend is the emptiness of unanswered questions. As a third-party observer, the causes of the tragedies of Job are played out before the reader.[5] The Sunday school class can analyze, philosophize, and memorialize the man of God. The preacher can proclaim the wonderful truths associated with the sovereignty of God, but there is the mother embraced by her friends as she cries out her unanswered lamentation: "Why, God, why? Oh, say it's not true! It can't be true! Not my baby, not my little girl." The loss suffered is so great that it crushes her ability to breathe.

In their book *All Our Losses, All Our Griefs*, Kenneth Mitchell and Herbert Anderson outline six major types of loss. *Material loss* is when some physical object or familiar surroundings are taken away. A *relationship loss* ends the opportunities to relate emotionally and physically with another human being. *Intrapsychic loss* is when an emotionally important might-have-been or plan is no longer possible. There are times a person suffers the loss of muscular or neurological functions; this *functional loss* is often associated with a loss of autonomy. Sometime subsequent to death, a person realizes that he is experiencing a *role loss*, viz. he is no longer a husband or father; he has lost that role. *Systemic loss* is when a loved one dies, and it dawns on the family that it will never be the same: "Our little ray of sunshine is gone."[6]

Life after death is not such a neat package that these losses can be dealt with one at a time and in a predictable order. They will come into the survivors' lives in no particular order, and they keep changing, or one day the bereaved will wake up and all six will be reality. When these life-changing events happen, whether Christian or not, a person experiences feelings of vulnerability and that the world, which was safe, is now unsafe.[7]

Sometimes the losses are finite because adjustments are made and function is restored, but there are times when the loss is chronic, permanent, because of its nature or because of decisions that are made, for example, "I'll never marry again."[8] Can a funeral anticipate these losses and assist the grieving to cope?

Coping with Loss

What does it mean to "cope with loss," and how can a funeral help with this? To *cope* means "1. to struggle esp. on fairly even terms or with some degree of success (usu. fol. by *with*). 2. to face and deal with responsibilities or problems (esp. calmly or adequately)."[9] Those to whom you will minister will struggle, but not on "fairly even terms." They will no doubt have *some* degree of success. During this emotional roller coaster and disruption of their "normal lives," they will need to face and deal with their responsibilities. They may not do so calmly, but they must deal with them adequately so as not to further complicate their lives or the lives of others.

A funeral can help them cope in at least two ways: by informing and experiencing that they are not alone and by giving them hope that though they have had a huge loss, because of the resurrection of Christ, there will be a reunion! There will be weeks, months, of adjustments, new patterns to learn, and figuring out the new "norm," but by the grace of God, you and your church family can help the grieving avoid wandering into the Slough of Despond.[10]

Chaplains who often must keep their theology to themselves have discovered that the Lord opens doors through the "ministry of presence."[11] They arrive soon after the tragic event and only stand by while the first responders meet the immediate need. The chaplains who do not speak, who could not perform a medical procedure, were simply there. Later they discovered that just the fact of their presence helped calm the EMTs, the victims, and their families. Your beautiful flock, entrusted to you by the Great Shepherd, needs to see you while their brother is dying. They need to see you standing in the hall while the doctor does what she can to stabilize the patient and at those times when the only words she can say are "I'm sorry. We did all we could."

Then later, when you proclaim from the pulpit that God will never leave them, that the Good Shepherd has gone before them and is waiting for them and nothing in heaven or on earth can separate them from the love of God, they will be inclined to believe, because *you* were there.[12]

> O LORD, thou hast searched me, and known *me*. Thou knowest my downsitting and mine uprising, thou understandest my thought afar off. **Thou compassest my path and my lying down,** and art acquainted *with* all my ways. For *there is* not a word in my tongue, *but,* lo, O LORD, thou knowest it altogether. **Thou hast beset me behind and before, and laid thine hand upon me.** *Such* knowledge *is* too wonderful for me; it is high, I cannot *attain* unto it. **Whither shall I go from thy spirit? or whither shall I flee from thy presence?** If I ascend up into heaven, **thou art there:** if I make my bed in hell, behold, **thou art there.** *If* I take the wings of the morning, *and* dwell in the uttermost parts of the sea; **Even there shall thy hand lead me, and thy right hand shall hold me.** If I say, Surely the darkness shall cover me; even the night shall be light about me. Yea, the darkness hideth not from thee; but the night shineth as the day: the darkness and the light *are* both alike *to thee.* For thou hast possessed my reins: thou hast covered me in my mother's womb. (Ps. 139)

You must also tell them that the "God Who is there" is also the Resurrection and the Life.[13] That thief known only as Death has already been defeated, and all of creation is waiting for and anticipating the crowning act of the resurrected Christ, which includes Him raising their loved ones from the dead.[14] For tonight, after the funeral, when family and friends have returned to their own homes, that widow will be lying in a half-empty bed, that mother will walk by the child's empty room, and the loneliness and grief will overwhelm them like a flood. It is then that God will speak peace to them. "Child of God, I am here. Dear one, your child, *our* child, is with Me, and one day, very soon, there will be such a glad reunion."

But what if in that memorial service the emphasis is placed on the details of the man's work and the things he enjoyed? I have had funeral directors tell me that "the message of the dash" has been popular, that is, the dash between the year a person was born and the year he died. The life the person lived was what was viewed as important and rehearsed. In contrast, years ago, I attended the funeral service of a cult member, and they glorified the grave because in that "victory," all of the sufferings were over. Where is the comfort in either of these messages when there is no hope given of the future? My dear Timothy, assure your flock that the God of the universe is present with them both now and in the days ahead. Proclaim the victory of the cross *and* the resurrection! These are the two foundational truths that will enable the brokenhearted to have hope for today and cope with tomorrow.

The Value of a Funeral for the Living

Besides the immediate family, there will be two kinds of hearers in the funeral service: those who need to be confirmed in their faith and those who need to be confronted with their unbelief.[15] They may have avoided thinking about their mortality in the past, but your funeral congregation cannot deny the reality of it today. They have drowned out the Spirit of God with noise and activity, but for a few minutes, under the sound of your voice, when it comes to their mortality, their faith will be confirmed or their unbelief will be confronted.

Family and friends come to the ones who have experienced loss. They want to experience together those rituals of their beliefs that bring comfort, so they "commission" someone to speak for them and to them.[16] At a memorial service, you may feel obligated to spend all the time rehearsing the man's or woman's accomplishments. The family wants a community memory that will help through the process of grieving.[17] This person was their loved one, and the family wants everyone to know what good she did for her family, the community, or an institution. It is right and wise to honor those to whom honor is due, but to spend thirty minutes on her good deeds and ten on matters of life, death, and eternity is to neglect the needs of those still living. The answer to this dilemma is balance and creativity.

The family can create a display for the family visitation time. Photographs of important events, plaques of recognition, perhaps a piece of furniture or a quilt made by the loved one's father or mother would make a valuable and personal statement. Many funeral services include a DVD of submitted pictures with music background to be played during visitation and before and after the service.[18] Encourage the family to be thinking of tangible ways to honor Mom other than reading a litany of accomplishments. For example, a third of the time of the service can be dedicated to "this was her life" and "this is how the family loved her."[19] Then it is time to lift up Jesus Christ, the God of all hope, Who can meet the family's needs today, tomorrow, and for eternity.

Communicating the brother's or sister's salvation testimony and what led to it confirms the faith of the saints. Reading the Word of God and proclaiming the Gospel gives assurance to those who have trusted Christ but who perhaps on this day need assurances—not from you but from God! We have already considered 1 Corinthians 15 and John 11. These are wonderful texts to assure the saints. You will find more suggested texts in chapters 6 and 13. Remember that the Apostle Paul said, "Faith comes by hearing and hearing by the Word of God" (Rom. 12:17). Faith and hope are traveling companions in Scripture; carry them into the pulpit.[20]

When it comes to the unbeliever, the man without faith, this is not a time to attack him but to lead him to the well of living water. You can state the obvious without shaking your finger in his faith. "It could be today, dear friend, you have once again thought about your mortality and doubts. God's Word has answers for you as well." I have heard messengers claim they know what the departed would say to their friends if they could. I am not comfortable doing that. How can I prove I have inside information? I could say, "There is a man whose words from eternity are recorded for us. His concern for his family is evident, when he said, 'Send Lazarus to my father's house: for I have five brethren that he may testify to them.'"

This ritual we call a funeral will address the fact of death and offer an opportunity to develop encouraging memories by the community's presence and a common place for the expression of grief.[21] As you prepare for the public service and the visits leading up to and following it, follow the exhortation of Jude, so you can "make a difference." Build yourself up by studying the Book, practice Holy Spirit praying, keep yourself in the love of God and look for His mercy. You will need this preparation to have discernment as to when to show compassion to the saints and when to confront the lost.[22]

The Gift of the Church at the Time of Loss

Many times I have heard how the church family, not just the pastor, has ministered to those who are grieving. Some of them are close friends; others are simply a face they passed in the hallway. The church is a body, and when one member is hurting, the whole Body feels the pain.[23] God in

His wisdom has enabled the Body to minister to one another in so many ways, and especially when there is a death. Consider the possibilities of how your church can minister to one another.

Death, as the "King of Terrors," sometimes causes the survivors to distance themselves from the reality that their loved one is gone. John tells us "perfect love casts out fear."[24] When you have a loving congregation who embraces the ones who are grieving, this helps the family walk through the valley of the shadow of death because they are not alone.

"Grief comes in waves."[25] Catherine Sanders, in her book *Grief: The Mourning After,* lists five phases of grief. First, there is shock, then awareness of loss, followed by conservation and withdrawal. With the help of the family of God, those who are grieving can go on to the fifth phase of healing and renewal.[26] Perhaps they can and will make it on their own, but what an amazing ministry the church can have by coming alongside this family who is hurting.

Prepare your congregation for these times with solid, biblical teaching on suffering, compassion, and the ministry of the Word and the Holy Spirit, along with the sovereignty of God. Helping survivors can be difficult, but it is not impossible. They will find family members are sometimes numb and in shock. Their grief can become intense, filled with thoughts of fear, guilt, confusion, and anger, and they need a child of God to come alongside just to listen. Sometimes the anger bleeds into rage, and this can be frightening, but it is not uncommon. They will hear the question "why?" over and over again. These are not times to quote clichés or try to discern the answers; they are times to be compassionate, to be there, to listen, to pray, console, and share Scripture that has been meaningful to you and appropriate for the occasion (1 Thess. 4:18).[27]

Sometimes your church members will be present before the loved one passes and may have opportunity to minister to him or her. Teach your church members the Five Rs of caring for the dying. Remember your limitations—you cannot repair their hearts. Recognize the power of your presence—just being there is helpful. Respect the person's values—some will want to fight; some are ready to go. Reinforce (respect) the person's rights to make decisions regarding medical care, visits, and so on. Reminisce about the past: if the person can communicate, ask him about the things important to him—and then listen![28]

You will want to get resources into the hands of your church family that not only will be helpful to them when they walk through this valley but for them to pass on when appropriate. Wally Stephenson, a missionary with the Association of Baptists for World Evangelism, has published several booklets, for example, *Helping a Friend Who Is Grieving*; *Helping*

Friends and Family of an Unbeliever Who Dies; *Questions Children and Adults Ask about Greif and Death*; and others.[29] More resources are provided in "Resources" at the end of the book and in the bibliography. You will want to establish a supply readily available for you and your congregation to read and distribute.

There are going to be members of your congregation and others to whom you will minister over the years who will make different choices as to how to remember and honor their loved ones. Some will choose to use the services of the funeral home and you; others will opt to do no more than make final arrangements for the burial of the body or cremains. It would be my preference for the reasons stated earlier to provide an opportunity for the family, the church, and friends to walk through this together. Regardless of the decision, you can still communicate the presence of God and the hope of the resurrection. You will be able to proclaim this either publicly or in the privacy of the family's home. Either way, be prepared.

CHAPTER THREE

THE PATTERNS OF FUNERALS

In every funeral or memorial service you attend, you will discover an atmosphere of hope or hopelessness. In the service where the presence of God and the hope of the resurrection are believed and proclaimed, you will sense hope. In the service where God is not present in the hearts of those grieving and there is no trust in the risen Savior, there will be hopelessness. As perhaps you have stated in your worship services, there are only two kinds of people: saved and lost—those with hope and those who are hopeless. This is also true at the funeral.

> Wherefore remember, that ye *being* in time past Gentiles in the flesh, who are called Uncircumcision by that which is called the Circumcision in the flesh made by hands; That at that time ye were **without Christ,** being aliens from the commonwealth of Israel, and strangers from the covenants of promise, **having no hope,** and **without God** in the world: But now in Christ Jesus ye who sometimes were far off are made nigh by the blood of Christ. (Eph. 2:11-13)

I have attended or officiated at funerals where hope was communicated through tears. This was a time not of blindness to the reality of death but of the joy and confidence of those who trust in a risen Savior. They have the hope that their loved one is absent from the body and present with the Lord. There is the hope of a reunion. The atmosphere is sometimes calm, sometimes festive. Then, I have been to funerals where the mourners distanced themselves as far as possible from the casket. You sense their hopelessness because they are in reality lost. There have also been times when presumptions of the eternal state of the loved one are made. "He's better off." "He's no longer suffering." "He's gone to be with Mother." There is no confidence in their voices; there is only the presumption that what they believe is true. One time I walked into a visitation hour, and it appeared to be almost a ruckus. The family and friends were glad he was gone "because the old man was such a tyrant!" This was not a mood of hope but a mood of relief from their father's tirades and demands. How sad. How hopeless!

The above is what I have observed in my limited view of funerals in the Midwest. Through the testimonies of missionaries around the world, I want you to note that the conclusions are the same whether in the States or across the oceans. Listen to their accounts.

Funerals around the World

Chad

When thinking about the funeral customs in Chad, the major thing that stood out is the "place mortuaire"—the gathering of friends and loved ones to the home of the family of the deceased. They will come to comfort the grieving family and come in large numbers. Some will come for an hour, some for several hours, some for several days, weeks, or months. I have seen the courtyards of the grieving family filled with large numbers of people. Unfortunately the comforters will need to eat and drink, so the grieving family will have to provide bread and hot sweet tea for all the guests several times a day. There is no idea of saying, "Thank you for coming, but we have to eat, or sleep." That doesn't mean they don't eat—they will eat the same bread and tea—but nothing more. They may sleep, but in the presence of the guests. During the long hours, the guests will sing hymns of Christian songs of comfort—all by heart—or they will bring their own hymnals. Most believers in Chad have a small handy hymnal that they sing from since the church has no hymnals of its own.

Among the unbelievers, wailing and beating the chest is common. The Christians would not do this, and those who did were looked down on. They were not to cry. Early missionaries had taught believers not to cry at funerals because we are told in Scripture that we should "sorrow not, even as others which have no hope" (1 Thess. 4:13). I have heard some believers confess that they cried when hearing that someone died and admitted that they shouldn't have.

I have heard that in unbelieving families there is a cruel mockery of those who are grieving. One man told me that he saw a man get on the back of the grieving husband or father and ride him like a horse. I'm not sure how that comforted the poor guy, but perhaps the thinking is to take his mind off the self-pity and generate an angry attitude in order to better handle the situation? I know that there is a certain fear of approaching the body of a person who has just died. The thinking is that the spirit of the dead is still there and there is a certain danger. Of what, I do not know. In any case, children are not allowed in the room of a person who has just died for this very reason.

Also in Chad, due to the heat, the body is buried directly after the funeral. In fact, no one leaves until the last shovelful of dirt is packed down on the body. The hole is dug and the dirt put back on top by the young men that come to the funeral. During the grieving gathering at the family home, there will be someone from the church who will give a short meditation from time to time. It would not be unusual for there to be two or three or more meditations a day and that for two or three days before the funeral. The Gospel was often preached to those who came. It was a good opportunity.[1]

Chile

The Chilean culture like most other Latin countries is to normally bury the person within twenty-four hours. Usually the day the person dies there is a viewing in the house or maybe the local church, and then the funeral is done at the gravesite.

The one Christian funeral I did, I was asked to do the funeral about four hours before the funeral at the graveside, and I shared it with another Chilean pastor who was a family friend. The general flow of the funeral was a couple close friends spoke, some family members spoke, a couple people sang an old church song, and then the other Chilean pastor and I spoke for about ten to fifteen minutes each. There was one more song after that, a prayer, and then the people were dismissed.[2]

France

The only thing here in France that I remember as being different is the color red; red is considered inappropriate apparel for those who come to the funeral. Wearing red is an insult to the grieving loved ones. I suppose red is identified with joyful or lighter occasions and is not fit for funerals. I remember seeing one missionary lady wearing red at a funeral, and though some would have excused her because she was not French, I heard echoes of others who thought it was inexcusable. For the number of years she had been on the field, she should have known better.[3]

Mexico

I work in Poza Rica, Veracruz, México. All over Mexico, the person that dies must be buried in twenty-four hours. Most Mexican funerals, the men are there for the wake. They stay all night playing cards and getting drunk. With Christians the alcohol is absent but mainly believers stay up with the bereaved to make the loss a little easier and show love to the family. However, my wife's death was handled very differently and scores of people cooperated.

    I advised the church that though she went to be with the Lord on Sunday afternoon, the burial wouldn't be until Wednesday to give opportunity for my children to all get here and to advise the undertakers to prepare her body to last. In the funeral home, we would have a religious service Monday night, Tuesday night and Wednesday before the burial. The funeral parlor had walls that could be opened up into another room. I think that there were at least three hundred at each service and viewing. We had worked with the Totonac Indians, two hours from Poza Rica. They brought their orchestra and stayed through the burial.

    When we arrived at the cemetery, another burial was in session, and I told everybody, "Be respectful and don't disturb them." The Catholic priest was there and said very little, nothing to console the family. They had a group of mariachis, orchestra and singers, like at a dance. I asked the orchestra from the mountains to wait until they were through but to begin immediately. The people waited and listened to the testimonies and the Gospel songs and commented to me that they observed the difference and that there was much love displayed to me and the family. I was at the burial spot the day after and had an opportunity to witness to part of the family, who commented, "What a difference in the hope expressed because the priest did not give any hope in what he said."

Other burials have singing, testimonies and prayers for those left behind. I have been to burials of several Catholics and what wailing goes on because there is no hope of seeing their loved ones in heaven.[4]

Mexico—Another View

When we first receive the news of a deceased loved one, the minister is expected to visit the home of the family and stay with them throughout the rest of the day and even night. If he does leave later in the early morning, the family would usually expect him to come back to their home and spend the next full day with them, comforting them, and holding short services throughout the day which include prayer, songs, Scripture reading, and a Bible devotional.

Some of the people from the congregation get together and join the family in their grief and cook food for the surviving family and all the guests. A shorter time between death and burial is usually preferred. A day or two is more common than three or four. The church, along with some family members, make arrangements to have flowers ordered, have *cafe de olla* (coffee on the pot—black coffee sweetened with raw sugarcane sweetener) and serve *pan dulce* (sweet pastries) at all times.

There is always a fund that is started right away to help with all the unexpected expenses. The family expects the pastor to guide them through their time of grief and separation and requests that he help making plans for the services. They often request that the Gospel be preached very clearly at the wake and the funeral service, which most often is held at the church with the body of the deceased present, and also at the interment. Guitars are taken to the graveside service and played along as the group sings the deceased's favorite songs. There is often an extended time for the sharing of testimonies. Some special music as well is presented at different times, and an elaborate meal is served after all the services conclude at the church or home of the family.

Because of the Catholic traditions, the pastor must not assume that everyone will be supportive of a Christian religious ceremony, so he must be sensitive and very careful not to promote a denomination or unnecessarily bring up topics of common disagreement. The Gospel message will usually be well accepted by everyone, even those of a Catholic persuasion.[5]

Myanmar

I can give some of my experiences from a very different view of funeral services in Chin State and Myanmar. We keep the dead body in the house until the funeral. We normally keep the body for three days.

We have a Comforting Service every night where we preach the Gospel and about heaven and hell, because there are many unsaved people who come every day and night to the deceased's home. Relatives, neighbors, and friends take advantage of the opportunity. On the third or funeral day we have a service at the house, then proceed to the cemetery on foot. It is a long service with preaching, singing, praying, and telling a brief biography of the deceased one.

At the cemetery, we sing one farewell hymn, read the Bible, pray, and commit to the ground/earth with prayer, then sing the Doxology with the Amen.

That funeral evening, the youth group takes the Comfort Service and makes tea with the bereaved family. The following evening service is led by our women's group, and they have a tea party, too.

So, when one dies it takes about five days of the matter.[6]

Spain

Because of the strong Catholic influence, it's hard to define what an evangelical funeral would be like. The law requires that within twenty-four hours of the death, the body must be disposed of, since no embalming is done. The body is usually washed and wrapped in linen cloth. If there is an open casket, sometimes you'll see the head wrapped in linen to keep the mouth closed. If the person dies at home, which happens less now that there are more residencies for the elderly, the police must be called, and a doctor must pronounce the person deceased. When someone dies in the hospital, they may stay in the hospital's *tanatorio* (which is a place for the wake), or if the family has another place designated, the body will be sent there. Most cemeteries also have these *tanatorios*, along with a crematorium.

The custom used to be for the family to stay with the body for the twenty-four-hour time span, but this is changing. The whole family is usually there until 11:00 P.M. or midnight and then returns the next morning. Funerals are usually within that twenty-four-hour period, so they can be as early as 8:30 A.M. or as late as 10:00 P.M.

Very few cemeteries have in-ground burials. Many Spanish municipal cemeteries have a system where a coffin is inserted in a recess or niche (rather than buried in the ground). This niche can be rented for a predetermined number of years. The remains are interred in the niche, and once the period expires, the body is moved to a common burial ground. There are also private cemeteries that would be more like cemeteries in the US, but these can be expensive. Each cemetery has different procedures, periods available, and prices. Some require a family member to go to the cemetery to witness the transfer of the body to a different niche. This is why so many are finding it easier to be cremated. Many people in Spain have "death insurance." You pay a small amount each month, and then when you die, the insurance company takes care of everything. They take care of the body, the death certificate, the funeral, the flowers, the announcements, the coffin, and the burial or cremation. With cremation, the ashes are usually picked up the next day at the funeral home.

Most funeral homes are set up for Catholic funerals. We have attended several. What is interesting is that in many cases, the priest doesn't know the deceased. If that person has been baptized, no matter what kind of life he lived, he is on his way to heaven.

The evangelical funerals I have attended have been varied. Sometimes we are able to obtain the use of the chapel, and we can have a regular kind of service where hymns are sung, and someone can give a eulogy. Often the time is limited, so it's hard to do too much. Sometimes we are forced to have a graveside service (if there is a grave) after the body has been interred because the gravediggers are standing by and can become quite impatient. It's quite a sight to see. The flowers are stuffed into the grave or niche, and then dirt is piled in. Many graves hold three to four bodies, so the coffin is placed on the top of the previous one, and all the names are engraved on the gravestone, which is level with the ground.

Usually the next Sunday or a few days after the funeral, a memorial service is held at a church. At that time there is an opportunity to give a more formal eulogy and preach a Gospel message, which is what the deceased has usually asked for. Catholics are required to have a Mass for the dead one week after the death, so oftentimes we will have our service one week later so that Catholic family members will attend.[7]

Taiwan

Taiwanese funerals are a little complex. To them, they believe that the body is very important for the afterlife. After they die, they become a god (it differs some depending on their religion). Once they become a god, they need their children's worship, so they can have things in the next life. So, you see people burning special "afterlife money" as a way of giving it to their ancestors. As I understand it, each ancestor keeps some and passes it on to the one before him, and so on.

In Taiwan, funerals have become a little more difficult because nearly everyone must now be cremated because of a lack of burial spaces. The price of a cremated funeral is subsidized by the government. Although it is against their traditional beliefs, nearly everyone is now cremated. The cremation process begins with the family bowing in worship and praying to the body before and after it is cremated. Then they take it (if they can) to a mountainside where there's a good view and good surrounding environment, e.g., *fēng shui*. That way they can enjoy the view and come out as they please.

Traditional burial sites are shaped rather like a small porch, with a couple of holes to let the family put water in for their afterlife needs. They often put flowers on the site, and they are supposed to put food out monthly. Most now offer the food only yearly, and after they've offered it, they eat it themselves. In Taiwan, nearly a whole month is given to the worship of their ancestors each year. Part of that month involves a special day to go clean the tomb, dump alcohol on it for them to drink, and put lit cigarettes on it for them to smoke. Apparently, the process is rather scary, and many people do not like to remember the first time they were forced to help with it.

Christians have completely rejected all these practices, but they often get pressure from family members to participate. This is often a reason why people refuse to become Christians. They believe the Bible but don't want to stand up to the family displeasure and pressure.[8]

Ukraine

Usually there is a string of mourners that slowly walks down the street while a small motley band plays a dirge. The people are walking, and a few are carrying the open coffin (wooden box) up high (on their shoulders). The dead person is visible as they go down the street. I have seen this right in front of our house. Sometimes a cart is pulled by a tractor, and sometimes the coffin is taken away by a small bus assigned for the purpose. If the people had a little money, an old truck might be used.

Each time I am struck by the straightforwardness compared to most funerals in the States. I remember the shock I felt at witnessing my first funeral here. There are grim reminders such as hearing the nails being hammered into the coffin's lid, seeing the open grave, and watching the hole being filled in as soon as the last Amen is said. The grave was dug with shovels, and the hole in the ground is before you as you approach the spot. There is a big mound of dirt and a few cemetery workers waiting like hawks for the end. At the end, some relatives throw in a clod or three—making a loud noise on the wooden box. Before mourners can even get away, the workers (apparently paid by the job) start shoveling dirt back into the hole. It seems undignified to Americans, but our funerals would seem strange to them, especially the waste of enormous amounts of money.

Most Ukrainians are Russian Orthodox by tradition. A typical funeral service starts in an apartment. A Russian Orthodox priest comes, for a fee, and "seals" the dead. She was recognized by the Orthodox Church and is safely on her way to heaven and has the church's paper seal taped to her forehead to prove it. I am not joking; this is seriously how they do it. I was told that if your faith wasn't much, the family can pay a fee and the priest will put a stamp of an Orthodox cross on your tombstone and that guarantees you into the Kingdom. When the graveside part is done, they invite the attendees for a meal at home or some eating place. Beware, many have alcohol here.

A note from another missionary friend here said this about a funeral they went to: the husband had brought with him holy water to sanctify the grave, coins to place in the coffin with her, a loaf of bread and salt to place on top of the grave, and little packets of candies and cookies to give the mourners who were present. All are customs of the Orthodox Church. The "service" was very brief, about fifteen minutes. They nailed the lid on the coffin and lowered it down with ropes. Each person threw in three handfuls of soil, and then the grave was filled in. Each family plot has low fences around them with a little table and bench. This is for Easter Sunday, as it is a custom for families to visit the graves and normally eat and drink there on that day. Forty days after the death, a Mass is held, and a meal is eaten to remember the departed.[9]

As we have noted, there is this deep contrast between the lost and the saved: for the lost, there is no hope, and for the believer, there is both comfort now and hope for the future. Dear Timothy, do not let your congregation leave the service, whether in the church, at the funeral home, or at the gravesite, without the hope of God's presence and the resurrection.[10]

Pattern of the Puritans

The Puritan, "American" version of funerals follows very much the pattern of experience today in nonliturgical services. The Puritans essentially "ruled" England for twenty years (1640-60).[11] Puritanism as a political power ended shortly after the death of Oliver Cromwell, Lord Protector of the Commonwealth of England, Scotland, and Ireland. Soon the Episcopacy and the Prayer Book were brought back into church life under Charles II.[12] But then Calvinism, through the medium of Puritanism, found its liberty in the New World and with it brought its form of dealing with death.[13] In the seventeenth century, Scotch Presbyterianism and English Puritanism combined to formulate their principles in doctrine, discipline, and worship. These carried over into the Congregational and regular Baptist churches of the British Empire and the United States and found their expression in theology and church life.[14] Now you will see, as Americans are wont to do, that the Old World Puritan approach to death was modified in the New.

Although Puritans worshipped within the Church of England, they wanted to change it. They promoted "greater simplicity in services, greater emphasis upon the Bible and to make the sermon much more central."[15] Not finding the liberty they sought, at least twenty thousand left for America between 1628 and 1640.[16] It is within the church life of the American Puritans that we see a major change in dealing with death.

While still in England, among the Puritans, an excessive display of sadness was to be avoided. Interment was speedy and simple. The body was clothed in white flannel. Prayers over the dead were superstitious and idolatrous. To wear black was an "artificial form of sadness" and hypocritical. Funeral services were without singing or reading or any kind of ceremony. They would simply commit the dead to the grave "with gravity and sobriety with the fear of God and hatred of sin which causes death."[17]

Non-Englishmen mocked and criticized the Puritans for their profane manner of burying their dead. It seemed to them that they were simply throwing the dead into the ground like dogs. When in control of the government, the Puritans took steps to move the care of the dead from the religious sphere to the hands of the civil authorities to distance themselves as far as possible from the papist practices.[18]

Early New Englanders followed their English pattern, but later, more and more Puritan funerals were conducted with elaborate and formal ritual.[19] By the late 1600s, funeral sermons were preached on the day of the burial with more eulogizing—some even misrepresenting the dead and misleading the living by flattery.[20] As the colonies grew wealthier, mourners began receiving memorial rings, scarves, and gloves. The showiness and expense offended the old Puritan leaders, and several efforts were made to limit these practices. The Massachusetts government enacted in 1741 a fine of fifty pounds for distributing wine and for excessive giving of gifts other than gloves to pallbearers and clergy. Bell ringing was also limited.[21]

However, with the Great Awakening, four major changes took place:

> An increase in religious enthusiasm by the believers, death changes from a horrible means to an end to an event truly looked forward to as a release from life's struggles, sermons celebrated the individual rather than focusing on the loss to the community and death's heads on gravestones gradually were

replaced with more pleasant, angelical figures, complete with wings.[22]

As a result of the religious revival sweeping across Europe and the Great Awakening of America, the churchyard became a part of the community. The burial ground was near and was a daily reminder of deceased family and friends and of the finality of death. The church sexton cared for the grounds, and the graveyard was an extension of the church community.

> Throughout the stages of American history, we can witness how the harshness of daily life became more tempered. The influx of colonists improved chances of survival of the community, the more traditional influences of Europe, and with the hope for rewarding life after death.[23]

Contemporary Funerals in My Community

The majority of my service for the Lord has taken place in two Ohio cities. Over the last forty years, there has been a gradual change in the character and content of the funerals I have attended and, in some ways, those I have officiated. Among the ones I have observed, most have been, as my Spanish missionary friend called them, Evangelical. Because in the following chapters you will learn my approach, I will describe the disappointing changes I have observed.

One of the significant changes has been in the "person of focus." In the early years, the congregants were immediately taken into the presence of God. This is not to say there was not a eulogy or testimony of the life of the departed brother, but he took a back seat to the God of all hope. The songs that were sung, the Scriptures that were read, the prayers that were offered, and the message that was given all pointed to "the God Who is here," and the Gospel of Christ was clearly proclaimed. No one left the service or the graveside without hearing of the hope of God's presence and the resurrection of the One Who died for their sins. This approach communicated that God was there for the mourners now and that there was a confident assurance of a glad reunion in the resurrection of their loved one.

We have moved from a memorial service to a "memorializing" service—not unlike the latter changes in the Puritan funerals. The majority of the services are spent in eulogizing the departed. You will hear a great deal about her accomplishments and her passions. Much will be said about what she meant to those who have survived. Let me be clear: I am not suggesting that the deceased brother or sister be ignored, but it seems to me that we have rewritten John the Baptist's goal in life to "we must increase; He must decrease." A couple of comforting songs are sung by either a soloist or the congregation, and then "the Gospel" is preached.

"The Gospel" is put in quotes because, sad to say—disappointing, really—the Gospel is only referred to by the term. Heaven is spoken of quite often. Grandpa is now in the presence of Jesus; there is no more pain or suffering, and "he would want you to know that you need to trust Christ." However, the Gospel is rarely proclaimed. I am not sure why it seems inappropriate to talk about the fact "that Christ died for our sins according to the scriptures; and was buried, and that he rose again the third day according to the scriptures" (1 Cor. 15:3-4). You will remember that without the death, burial, and resurrection of Christ, there is no hope, and though we "sorrow not as those who have no hope," it is left as a mystery in the heart of the departed loved one. As you may have guessed, this is one of the pressing reasons why I have pursued writing this book. We have kept the label of the Gospel but have failed to proclaim it at the one event where it is needed the most! O Timothy, this ought not to be!

Funerals Where You Live

Before we leave this topic, and, I hope, before you officiate your first funeral, I want to encourage you to be an observer at funerals in your community. My culture is pure Midwest, and there may be expectations in your field of service of which you ought to be aware. It might be something as simple as not wearing red. It might be a family or even a church tradition that a certain funeral home has been used for generations.

Get to know your local funeral director. We will consider this person more in a later chapter, but she may save you some embarrassment if you simply ask a few questions regarding traditions in your community. Spend time with one of the deacons who has been in the church a long time, and seek his counsel as to church and family expectations. Understand that I am not suggesting you alter your convictions, but a brief conversation with a trusted servant of God may enable you to have a greater and unhindered ministry to the saints entrusted to you. Today I wish I had spent more time with Ron, Bob, Jim, Mike, Ben, Dan, or Maynard—good and godly men who faithfully served their churches and knew the people. I also had the privilege of serving under five pastors, men of God: Eldon Weaver, Timothy Crown, Fred Crown, Richard Pettitt, and David Melton.

I learned from them by observation, but surely it would have been wiser on my part to have spent an hour or more on this ministry with one of them, or when I was on my own, I could have spent time with a pastor who had been in the community a long time, such as Richard Snavely, Gene Milioni, or James Dennis. I mention their names because I want to encourage you to think of those living in your field of service. Now stop reading and call one of them—ask for an hour of his time over a coffee or a Coke, and be ready to ask and then listen to his answer to this simple question: "What can you tell me about funerals in our town?"

CHAPTER FOUR

WALKING WITH THE SHEEP AS THE SHADOWS LENGTHEN

I was standing, leaning on the wall really, just outside a room on the sixth floor—the floor dedicated to hospice. A longtime member of our church and also a dear friend lay dying in that room. We had served the Lord together in our church for more than twenty years. He had been a member of it for nearly fifty years. We'd had the privilege of walking through the experiences of his life: weddings, deployments, births of grandchildren, celebrations of life, deaths of loved ones, and multiple hospitalizations for him, his wife, and other family members. We never talked about all those times of happiness or sorrow. Neither of us was keeping track—they just came one by one, and we walked those valleys and mountaintops together. I was not thinking about them at that time; I was just praying for him and his family as I quietly leaned on the wall of that familiar hallway. As I was lost in thought and prayer, one of his sons came out of the room, and he said, "You've always been here for us. Thank you."

God had called my wife and me into the ministry forty years earlier. We spent four years in college, raised our family, experienced our times of highs and lows, and God had always had someone for us during those times. It was not until that day, though, that it dawned on me—this is ministry. The man in that room had heard me preach at least thirty-five hundred times, but at that moment, the most important part of my ministry to him was simply being there, leaning against the hospital wall, praying. Dear Timothy, you must study the Book, you must work on agendas, spend hours in committee meetings, fold bulletins and knock on doors, but when your sheep are celebrating a wedding or suffering in the hospital or dying at home, you will want to be—you must be—with them. They have the Good Shepherd Who will never leave them, it is true, but they need their "under-shepherd" standing with them, praying with them, weeping with them, especially as they walk through the shadows.

Develop a Relationship with Them before They Need You

Depending on which survey or article you read, it appears that the average time a pastor stays in one church is between five and seven years, and some stay as short a time as one to two years.[1] If what I was told in Bible college is true, that it takes five years to get to know your congregation and for them to know you, we have a problem.[2] If you are a pastor in certain denominations, you have very little control as to how long you will be in your parish. The majority of us will not be like Laban Ainsworth, whose pastorate in Jaffrey, New Hampshire, lasted for seventy-six years![3] However, if you are going to have an effective ministry in the life of your flock, and if they are going to trust you and hear you, then you must begin developing a relationship with them right away.

Paul Lamey, pastor and graduate of the Master's Seminary in Sun Valley, California, lists the following principles of a long pastorate and, in my opinion, gives you the opportunities you need to develop your relationship with your congregation:

> Principle 1: Preaching through books of the Bible takes times and allows you to prepare the church for the hard experiences of life.
> Principle 2: Training the next generation of leaders will require you to get to know your people and cultivate men and women into leaders who will minister to their "little flocks" now and larger ones in the future.
> Principle 3: Shepherding the flock means you will be with them when they are suffering and rejoicing.
> Principle 4: Modeling an exemplary home life in submission to the Lord and His Word pictures for the church how you deal with loss as well as victories.
> Principle 5: As their under-shepherd you will protect them from false teaching and be there to minister the balm of Gilead when they are hurting.
> Principle 6: Staying in one place for a long time reveals a pattern of faithfulness and grants you the opportunities to be there to share in their joys and walk with them through the shadows.[4]

The bottom line is this: you must take the time to be with them in the trenches, not just preach to them from behind the pulpit.

Respond Quickly to Their Call

When I was in my early twenties, I was an assistant pastor and served in an interim capacity while the church searched for a senior pastor. In the middle of the night, I received a call from one of the men that his father had died. He was with him in the house. I remember thanking him for the call, said I would be praying for them, hung up, and went back to sleep. That, dear Timothy, is not shepherding the flock. I was acting like a hireling. My response should have been to quickly dress and go to their home. He was reaching out for help and comfort, and I was not there! I served in that church for another ten years, but I was never able to get past the surface things of life with that man. Perhaps it would have been different if I had gone to him in his time of need.

When a family member dies, whether suddenly or at the end of a long illness, it is never at a convenient time. You may be awakened in the early hours of a late night. You may be taken away from a family occasion or working in the garden. It could be you are in the depths of preparation for Sunday or on your way to an important meeting, but when you get this call, it must be no less important than a 911 call for a fire or police protection. Consider for the moment this scenario: The worship service on Sunday morning is about to begin, and you get a call from the hospital. Worshippers are in their seats; the prelude music can be heard down the hall. You hang up and look at your worship leader and tell him Brother Williams just died. Timothy, do not wait until you get that call. Think through it now. How can you be in two places at once? What will you do next?

Waiting with the Sheep in the Shadows

I finished the previous section last night. This morning I received a message that a man I had met many times and whose family regularly attends our church was in the hospital, and they feared he was near death. For a moment I thought of all the important tasks on my to-do list, but right then, they did not matter. I grabbed my coat and invited our assistant to come, and we traveled an hour to be with the family in their time of need.

Eight years ago, we received a call on a Wednesday from a family whose father had been in a horrible accident and was in critical condition. The church family would be coming for services in a few hours, but we needed to be at the hospital. As a missionary friend from the Ivory Coast used to say, "What to do?" You take a few minutes to call the leaders in the church to cover your responsibilities if you should not make it back in time, and you ask them to pray. Hopefully, you have studied ahead, so the family will have your full attention. Otherwise, you will be distracted while with them, and tonight, if you make it back in time, you will be serving a half-baked message to the flock.

Speaking of the family, sometimes they will be apologetic for calling you, knowing you are busy getting ready for upcoming services, but for their sakes, none of that matters. You are there, waiting with them in the shadows. If you are going to effectively minister to them, it will be helpful to understand what is going on in their hearts and minds.

Kenneth Mitchell and Herbert Anderson list a dozen emotions that people will experience in times of loss. When you arrive at the hospital or the home, you will see some or all of them played out before you. After the loved one dies, you can expect the emotions to come in a new wave: guilt, shame, loneliness, anxiety, anger, terror, bewilderment, emptiness, profound sadness, despair, and helplessness. "Grief is the clustering of some or all of these emotions in response to loss."[5] Before you walk into that room, you will begin to doubt whether you can minister to this family who sways back and forth from hope to despair. The fact is that in yourself, you have nothing to offer them. You cannot take away the hurt. You cannot hit replay. You cannot heal the sick. You cannot raise the dead. What you can do in the moments and hours ahead is point them to the God of all comfort Who is there. Your presence in that room is a declaration that the Lord is indeed there.

> Blessed *be* God, even the Father of our Lord Jesus Christ, the Father of mercies, and the God of all comfort; Who comforteth us in all our tribulation, that we may be able to comfort them which are in any trouble, by the comfort wherewith we ourselves are comforted of God. (2 Cor. 1:3-4)

Do not assume that those to whom you minister will face these hours and this day as you would. Every person is unique; however, there are three sources for the feelings associated with grief. There is the contemplation of the loss. There is the anticipation of the future without the husband or wife or child. There is also the anxiety of not knowing what their grief will be like in the future.⁶ You cannot anticipate all of these. You cannot successfully switch from the spouse sitting by the bedside in a state of numbness to the son in the waiting room who is overwhelmed with guilt for not being there for his parents or for angry words exchanged over the phone that cannot be taken back. You cannot, but the God Who is at the scene for the family is also there for you. Trust the Holy Spirit to guide you either to sit quietly by, to accompany a spouse to the kitchen for a cup of coffee, or to bring the children together to hold hands and pray. It is hard to know what to do while you are waiting.

What to Do While You Are Waiting

Waiting can be hard, tiring work. Sitting in a hospital all day waiting for the anticipated death of a loved one can be exhausting—physically, mentally, and spiritually. At other times, the loved one gradually gets worse over a period of days or weeks. Generally speaking, the closer death is, the more often you will visit, and the longer you will stay. There may be times you stop by their home or the hospital every few days. If there is more than one on staff, you can take turns. At times you may have one of the deacons or a Sunday school teacher stop by as well. As wonderful as that is, it is my experience that the family is looking for their pastor. Do not neglect this great work. "I was sick and ye visited me" (Matt. 25:36).

If it is a terminal and slowly progressing illness, a visit every few days may look like this. Whether in the home, the nursing home, or the hospital, make your visit brief; plan on staying no longer than ten minutes or so. The patient, as well as the family, is weary. If the person is at home, you will need to call first to make sure of a convenient time to come. As you enter, greet all who are in the room, and if the patient is alert, turn your attention to him. A little lighthearted dialogue is fine, but he expects and needs you to turn his attention to the God Who is there. Be prepared to read a few verses of Scripture, perhaps even just one. Read slowly and clearly (remember he is weary), make a brief comment, and then offer to pray. Communicate your love and the church's for the patient, and then excuse yourself. Better for him to wish you had stayed a little longer than to wish you had left earlier.

One more thought while you are in the home or visiting in the hospital or nursing home: remember your role as a pastor. You are not the family doctor. You may have medical training, but it is unwise, if not illegal and unethical, for you to offer a medical opinion. Your knowledge of the patient's condition is only superficial, and that is not why you have been called to the bedside.[7] You are there to provide spiritual help, not a diagnosis or prognosis. Your tools are the Word of God, prayer, and compassion.

What if death is imminent? What if you are going to be there for several hours? Know this first: just being there is a comfort to the family. You do not have to engage the family and the dying loved one in continuous dialogue or keep a monologue going. When you first arrive, check with the patient's nurse to let him know who you are and that you plan to be with the family. Next, you will want to greet the family members who are present and discern who is the actual or the acting "family patriarch"—he or she will be your barometer throughout the day or night as to when to engage the entire family in prayer and consolation.

As soon as is convenient for most of the family, and without getting in the way of the medical staff, either you or the "patriarch" can invite the entire family into the room. If there are just a few, you can circle the bed and read an appropriate Scripture. Then ask the family to join hands while you pray for the grace of God to sustain the family and thank Him for their loved one. Over the next few hours, you will find members who want to stay in the room and others who want to wait in the family lounge or stand in the hallway. It is here you will again need the Spirit's discernment whether to engage in conversation or simply find a chair in an obvious place to be available. It is fine to read a book or to work from a tablet or phone, but do not bring a briefcase full of work to spread out on the table in the waiting room. You are there for the family. That is your work at this time—waiting with the sheep in the shadows.[8]

What to Do after the Patient Has Died

Whether it marks the end of a lengthy illness or is the result of an accident that day, as soon as you are informed of the loved one's death, you are needed. If you are already with the family and loved one, you will see a variety of responses. Some will walk out of the room in defiance of the truth. An aged saint will stand by his sweetheart of fifty years, quietly patting her hand with a tear in his eye, but with an understanding that this unnatural event is all part of God's plan. A child may be confused, asking what happened and going from mom to dad to aunt or uncle wanting answers that no one is able to provide.

Then there is the unofficial patriarch, who slowly walks to the nurses' station to inform them that he thinks Mom has died. One or two medical personnel will come in to confirm what everyone knows and then will ask all to leave the room while they unhook the equipment. At that time, they will perhaps express their condolences to the family members standing outside, answer any questions they may have, and instruct them what needs to take place next, but that there is no hurry. Then they will walk away and leave the family in your care.

Invite the family to gather around the bed or room, you standing near the head. This is the time you can communicate your love for them and the one lying still beside you. If you experienced this in your own family, you might say, "I know a little about what you are experiencing right now," but if you have not, do not tell them "I know how you feel." It will always be appropriate, however, to say, "There is a God Who knows perfectly what you are feeling and is grieving with you. I believe His Word will be of comfort to you. I will read from Scripture." After you read the Scripture, pray for the family and thank the Lord for their loved one. Express again your love for them, let them know you will be there if they need you, and then back away and allow the family private time to grieve and to come to grips with their loss.

Now it is time again to wait. You may have to wait a few moments or an hour or more. This is not a time to hurry the processing of death. You are waiting nearby if someone wants to talk and to speak tenderly to the family as they leave one by one. Finally, you are there to help the patriarch with any arrangements, if needed. It may be that all the funeral home decisions have already been made, or it could be that no one was prepared and they do not have a clue as to what is next. If all is settled, stay as long as it seems helpful to the family, and then excuse yourself, making sure they know how they can contact you if needed. If nothing has been arranged, then it is time to sit down with the key members of the family and walk them through this valley step by step.

Typical Decisions That Need to Be Made before the Family Leaves

At this point, if you are not careful, you will become nothing more than what Jay Adams calls a "death technician."[9] You are not simply dealing with technical services; you are there as God's representative to minister to the grieving. One day either someone will be helping you walk through this valley or helping your spouse or children. You will want that person to be compassionate and understanding during this extreme moment of grief. Forget about your other pressing matters later that day. For the moment, this family needs your full attention as their shepherd.

Find a conference room or an empty waiting area, or if at home, the living room or kitchen table will give you a place to carry on a private conversation with the family members who have the responsibility of deciding on the care of their loved one's body. Depending on the circumstances (a death without medical personnel present or the patient's decision on donating his organs), most of the time, it will be necessary for the family to choose a funeral home before they leave. If the body is being transported to the coroner's office or a facility caring for donations, this decision may be postponed on the hospital's part. If the deceased had previously made funeral arrangements, then it will only be necessary to contact the office of the funeral director. This is something the hospital personnel will do for the family.

What if no decisions have been made? How will you be called on to help?

There may be times when the family will look to you and say, "Pastor, we've never done this before. Who do we call? What do we do?" Tread carefully, dear Timothy. You are about to be pulled into making a decision that belongs to the family and that may come back to bite you. There may be a social worker or hospital chaplain who could help the family through this, but they are looking to you. Make sure you are speaking to the "patriarch" of the family, the primary caregiver or friend who has a legal position with the deceased, for example, as executor of the will. Is the family sure that no prefuneral arrangements have been made?

This is when it will be helpful for you to be acquainted with several funeral homes in the community. You do not want to be accused of "sending business" to a friend, but you can list several funeral homes and their locations, perhaps share some knowledge of the directors, and inform if any of the funeral homes had cared for other church family members in the past. The decision is not yours to make, but the family will be appreciative of any direction you can give them. After passing on the information, let the family communicate their decision to the hospital staff.

It has been a long night. Everyone is tired and ready to get some rest—no matter how "restless" it will be. Unless the family has asked you, do not assume you will officiate the funeral. You can offer them your phone number; communicate that if they need anything, they are free to call; and then excuse yourself. If they have asked you to lead the funeral arrangements, this is not the time to discuss the details. Let them get their rest; there is plenty of time to work on the arrangements over the next several days.[10]

You have communicated to the family that there is plenty of time, because they do not need any more stress than what they have just experienced. For you, Timothy, the clock is ticking: service plans that you will care for, the church family to contact, family responsibilities—and Sunday is coming. The next nine chapters are designed to help you face all the preparations of which, for the most part, the family and church will be unaware but that you have to make. You can cut back on your stress and work over the next few days if you have enlisted and trained key people in your church to assist at this time. You do not have to do this alone, and you should prepare now by delegating to the Body the tasks that they are equipped to do and can do. This is a wonderful time for the Body to come alive!

 CHAPTER FIVE

PREPARATION
The Hours from Death to Good-bye

In Judaism and Islam, the dead are traditionally buried within twenty-four hours.[1] Rituals and traditions of mourning will follow. In the Christian faith, there is no clock ticking, but for you, Timothy, much must be accomplished in a brief time. Over the next few days, there will be multiple individuals or groups to call and with whom to meet. There will be a message and a service order to prepare. You will be answering questions and giving direction to the family, the church, and the funeral director. Officiating at weddings is spread over weeks or months—not so for the funeral. Where will you begin?

Hopefully, you have an instrument to inform the church family—a prayer chain or the church's deacons can expedite this. It is vital to engage the church in praying for and caring for those who are grieving, and it is, of course, what makes the family of God so wonderful when they join in each other's sorrow.[2] Some of the most difficult times of the church body are when one of the saints dies, but it can also be an experience that draws the church together by strengthening their bond to one another. In many ways, it will not be pleasant—it will even be painful—but I believe you will look back at this week as one when Christ was building His church.

The next three to five days will pass rapidly due to the many possible ways you will be called upon to minister to the grieving family, their relatives, and their friends. Perhaps your church has multiple staff members to whom you can delegate responsibilities. What a marvelous gift at this time! But what if the pastoral staff is just you? With a servant's heart, you can care for all of what needs to be done, but it is so much better to engage the Body—it is one of the reasons for which Christ designed His Bride. Let me walk you through this.

If another pastor has been asked to officiate the funeral, a variety of factors brought the family to that decision. Perhaps you just became the pastor of the church, and the previous pastor, who lives only a few hours away, buried their father, their mother, and a younger brother. Maybe they have a relative whom they have called on in these times. This is not the time to "protect your turf." Their pastor ought to give you a courtesy call to make sure you are fine with this arrangement—he may; he may not. Regardless of what he does, you will need to respect the family's wishes. However, there are other ways you and the church family can minister.

Open your calendar and review what is going on in your life and that of the church for the next week. Either later in the day the death occurred or the following day, you will get a call from the funeral director. He has met with the family (they may even be in the office when he calls), and he is confirming with you your availability for the funeral day and time. Many factors can create a challenge for you in this, but do your best to accommodate the family's wishes. They will be dealing with out-of-town guests' travel time, holidays, and weekends. The latter two can create extra costs from the funeral home, cemetery, and vault company. The family may be trying to avoid these expenses. Once the days and times of family visitation and the funeral have been established, you will want to disseminate that information to the Body.

Beyond this, it will be difficult to list what will happen step by step or chronologically. You are ministering to a family and a church that have just experienced the most unnatural event of their lives. Like many occasions in life, this reminds me of the man in the circus who spins plates on the tops of a dozen sticks. Each plate must be kept spinning and balanced—at the same time. Recently I toured our local 911 Center. There were a dozen individuals looking at six to eight screens each. Incoming calls are on one screen. Instructions to first responders are being typed onto another screen. Then there are screens for maps, local news, and so on. The person sitting in front of the screens with her eyes darting from one screen to another is just as calm as when you are reading your emails on one screen. She must be calm and controlled and clear. How does she do it? Instruction and practice help her, and they will help you, too. We will discuss all the possible activities you will be coordinating. You will need to switch from one screen to another as the days progress, but remember that you "can do all things through Christ, which strengtheneth you" (Phil. 4:13).

Call on the Family within Twenty-Four Hours

If possible sometime during the first day, assuming you will be officiating the funeral, set up a meeting with the family.³ You will want to meet with those who are responsible for making the arrangements for the deceased. It may be a spouse, children, a friend, or all of these. Ask them for an hour of their time, so you can discover their wishes for the funeral, memorial service, or celebration of life.⁴ After listening to them for a while, you will be able to discern their view of the service. Take with you your Bible, a pad of paper and a pen, the church calendar and phonebook, and perhaps a hymnal.

Begin your time with the family by ministering to them in their grief. This includes prayer, Scripture reading, and just letting them talk. Depending on how well you know them and knew the deceased, they may tell you about his last minutes, who was there, who was not, and "Oh, how we miss him!" This is *not* wasted time. Listen.

Gently turn their attention to the arrangements that have already been made with the funeral director. The days and times have been set, and to these you have already agreed. If they are planning on having the family visitation and the service at the funeral home, then you can focus on the service itself. Topics will include favorite Scriptures, hymns, family and friends' participation, congregational singing, and possibly a soloist or group to sing or play. They may offer these freely, or you may have to ask questions, for example, "Did your father have hymns that were especially meaningful to him?" "Do you want the grandchildren to sing one of them?" "Is there a brother or sister who likes to write poetry?" "Do you want a time when family or friends can share a story?" All the time you are asking these questions, you are listening and writing down the ideas.

As you can see from this, I am encouraging a very personal service. This will become a special memory for the family, and it also helps in the grieving process as a way to express their love for the deceased. To continue the personal theme, you can now shift to asking them to share a few stories about their loved one. This typically starts out slowly, and as one shares a story, it stirs the memory of another. By the way, you may hear similar stories while you are at the hospital in the waiting room. Take notes! These will be used during the reading of the obituary, which can be very dry and mechanical—more on this later. Sometimes you can use the stories as illustrations during the funeral message.

As your hour with the family is coming to a close, prepare them for your departure by thanking them for their input. "I will use what you have given me to design the service. Later I can either email you the order of service or call you to get your approval." You must keep in mind that this is the family's service—you are only guiding them through it. Some will give you carte blanche; others will want to be more involved. By working through the order of service and other funeral details, we have added another element that I believe needs to be in the funeral service: God is present, Jesus is alive and the personal element. This was their dad, their son, their loved one, and though it may be your "assignment" to make it all happen, it is very personal to them.

Prepare Them to Meet with the Funeral Director

It is very possible that the family will either ask you to meet with them and the funeral director or ask you what to expect. If you have not already, before your first funeral, set up a meeting with one or more of your local funeral directors. They are generally happy to discuss with you the decisions that need to be made by a family. It can be overwhelming. This is why preplanning a funeral has become a very valuable step. What a blessing it would be to the children if Dad had already made the arrangements and even paid for them. Today, this is not the case. They have called you because Dad just died, and it took them all by surprise.

If you Google "preplanning a funeral," you will find multiple websites to walk you through this. For now, here is some of the information the funeral director requires and just a few of the questions that the family will need to answer: personal data, including a Social Security number and military records, if a veteran; if it will be a burial or cremation; possible days for visitation; if there will be a funeral and/or graveside service; location of the funeral—church, funeral home, family home, or combination; what cemetary they want; if a military honor guard will be requested; how the family will travel to the gravesite—personal car or limousine; the pallbearer names; and who is responsible for paying for the services.

There will be the decisions as to the products and services to be purchased. This is another area where you can gently give some direction. These decisions are made at a time when the family is vulnerable—emotionally and physically worn out, feeling guilty, or wanting to do the best they can afford because of their love for Dad. For some of your families, money may not be an issue, so you can talk stewardship with them. For some of your families, this one event can create a very difficult hardship and may have them financially strapped for years to come. I am not trying to be crude but rather practical, and as I said, think stewardship.

Dad does not need the most expensive casket available. In a day or two, no one will see it ever again, and once they walk away from the gravesite, no mourners will remember whether it was stainless steel or oak. Then there is the question of the vault or grave liner. Perhaps some state laws require it, but most of the time, it is dictated by the cemetery. They are required to reduce the amount of maintenance of the grounds by supporting the ground around the casket.[5] Again, you do not need the most expensive; in fact, the least expensive will be just fine. As you know, no one will ever notice it or even see whether it is concrete, reinforced concrete, stainless steel, plastic, or bronze.

There is another place where expense can be saved and the family can be a good steward. The obituary informs the public regarding the death of the individual by way of newspapers and the funeral home website. No state laws require an obituary to be published; however, the funeral home will help the family file a death certificate with the state's office of statistics. If the decision is made to publish in the newspaper, understand that the family is paying for words—the more words, the more it costs. I would encourage the base amount of words. If family and friends read it, they knew him, and all that is required are the times and days of the services. If the public does not know him, it will only be idle curiosity, if they even choose to read it. There is no reason to write a brief biography and pay more for it.

Before we leave the topic of money, let us discuss your fee or the honorarium. This can be a very awkward conversation. I recommend you do not bring it up. This is the responsibility of the funeral director. However, if a family asks you what you charge, I hope you will say, "I do not charge for this." I have had a similar discussion with those I have counseled. I hope you can say what I have been able to say over the years: "Our church takes very good care of my family; there is no charge." That being said, you may receive a check from the funeral director—discreetly, I hope. You may have one of the family members press some money into your hand or enclose cash in a thank-you note. I have been given a few dollars up to nearly a week's salary. You will need to keep a record of this for your tax returns—it is considered income, not a gift. One of my favorite gifts was from a dear saint who is a wonderful cook—a huge pan of cinnamon rolls. There were enough to share with others. Let me share one more word of advice that I was given during a pastoral theology class. Our professor said, "When you get paid for a wedding, give that to your wife to spend on anything she wants. When you get paid for a funeral, put that towards buying a new suit." Wise counsel!

Practical Ways to Involve Your Church Family

Recently I had a brief conversation with my doctor, who is from Ethiopia, regarding funeral practices there. He related that as soon as there is a death, family and friends start pouring in and will stay from a few days to a month. It would be a huge, even impossible, expense, but the Christian community has a fund that everyone gives to, and when a death occurs, all the expenses of the funeral, housing, food, and so on are cared for out of that fund. The family is expected not to do or pay for anything. What a blessing that would be in our culture!

The death of one of the saints can be used of God to create unity within the church family, a closeness that they have not experienced heretofore. Do not let your congregation miss this opportunity to care for one another. How can the Christian community of your church come alongside to care for one of the families who is grieving?

You can begin formulating this mind-set before it is needed. Perhaps a series of messages on the "one another" passages will help lay the foundation.

- Love One Another: John 13:34,35, 15:12, 17; Rom. 13:8; 1 Thess. 3:12, 4:9; 1 Pet. 1:22; 1 John 3:11,23, 4:7, 11-12; 2 John 1:5
- Be Ye Kind One to Another: Eph. 4:32
- Bear Ye One Another's Burdens: Gal. 6:2
- Care One for Another: 1 Cor. 12:25
- Comfort One Another: 1 Thess. 4:18
- Consider One Another: Heb. 10:24

Then it is time to train your leadership, that is, the deacons and their wives. The first-century church counted on them to minister to the grieving families of the congregation (Acts 6). The apostles realized that caring for all the needs of the widows would surely overwhelm them and consume the resources they needed to preach and teach the Word. These couples are well respected by your congregation (Acts 6:3) and are no doubt gifted (Rom. 12:8). With a little direction and communication, you can "turn them loose" to love the family.

Their phone calls and visits to the family will go a long way in comforting the family, and as a couple, they can be invited into the home to meet various needs: child care, food preparation, transporting the family members to and from public transportation, rearranging furniture to accommodate guests, and so on. Just their presence in the home for a few moments can communicate that the church family cares and loves those who are suffering. Later these servants can lead the congregation in attending the visitation times or setting up the fellowship hall for a dinner and serving, and if the visitation times and funeral are at the church, these couples will become the "face of the church" by greeting and directing family and friends who come for the services. When the attendees have gone, these couples will be there to clean and set up the building for Sunday services. Your church leaders are setting the example and the pace for the rest of the congregation in many areas of church life; this is true also in times of suffering.

Not only will the family be ministered to by the church but others are also watching. I remember one funeral director telling me that of all the churches in town, our church always turned out in large numbers during the visitation times. How did he know? I never asked him, but a quick look at the funeral guest register confirmed what he had observed. Even directors need a church family, and when the Lord works in this man's heart regarding his spiritual life, where do you suppose he will start looking? We all lead very busy lives, but you can teach your congregation that a ten-minute stop at the funeral home on their way home from work can be very meaningful to those who are grieving. Some will stress over not knowing what to say. Assure them they do not have to be so concerned. A simple "I'm so sorry for you" and what I call a "holy hug"[6] will be more than enough. Can you imagine the impact on the suffering saints and the testimony to their unsaved family members as they are greeted over and over again by a couple dozen families from your church?

There are also times that the church family can be involved in the memorial service. This is especially true if it is held at the church. The ways can include the following: meeting florists dropping off arrangements; assisting the funeral director when he brings the body; turning lights on and off; turning up the heat; running the sound system (including recording the services); playing one of the instruments before, during, and after the service; providing a nursery or at least directing toward changing tables, and many other ways. Pastor, if you do not engage the church family, who will do these things? Many of the actions that need to be taken do not require special or trained skills. Lead the church in ministering to one another.

We will dedicate a chapter to this later, but let me mention another wonderful way in which many within the Body can serve. Often your church has shared a meal, and they have learned certain skills that can be used to care for the grieving family. With so many out-of-town guests and responsibilities and the fact that many do not feel like eating, the family may often neglect themselves and may not have anticipated their guests' needs. This is where the church family ought to be ready to step in. Most of the time, this will take place after the graveside service. Where can twenty to a hundred or more guests spend an hour or two together before they head back home? This can be held in your church's fellowship hall or gym. It is here where they can sit and visit and laugh and take care of physical, social, and emotional needs. Both family and friends will be very grateful that you provided this for them.

The services are complete, the meal is finished, and the family is ready to go home. Consider a few final ways you can minister to the saints. More often than not, there is a lot of food left over from the meal. With foam plates and plastic wrap, you can take care of the family for a couple more days. Pack up the extra food for them to take home, and use containers they do not have to return. The hinged containers (clamshell) work really well for this. A lot of flowers may be left from the funeral that can become a chore for the family, and at times they will leave more than you can use at the church or that will still look pretty by the time of the services. Nursing homes are glad to get these arrangements. They break them up into smaller arrangements for their dinner tables or to be delivered to the residents' rooms. This extra mileage gotten from a one to two hundred dollar arrangement is appreciated by the family. Then just before the families leave, offer to borrow their camera phones to take a group picture of the extended family. We all know that most of them will not be together again until the next funeral, and the family picture is a wonderful reminder of the time they spent together over these two or three days.

Sometimes we describe what the saints go through when a loved one dies as "bereavement." Paul wrote to the Thessalonians regarding the losses they had experienced. "But I would not have you to be ignorant, brethren, concerning them which are asleep, that ye sorrow not, even as others which have no hope" (1 Thess. 4:13). This does not teach, as the early Puritans believed, that there should be, would be, no mourning, but it is different from those who have no hope. Paul told the Corinthians that the "sting of death" is gone![7] However, they are still "bereaved."

What does it mean to be bereaved? It is used of a person who is greatly saddened at being deprived of a loved one at death. It comes from the late Old and Middle English of the twelfth century. It means "to deprive ruthlessly or by force, to take away by violence."[8] That is just what happened. It might have been an accident, a crime, an act of war, an illness or disease, or simply old age that caught up with Grandpa, but in our hearts and minds, we are now deprived of his company, his friendship, his life. Funerals are a time when your church family can shine with the love of Christ and the presence of God. Will they be ready? O Timothy, get them ready!

CHAPTER SIX

THE FUNERAL SERVICE
A Celebration of Life or a Preparation for Eternity?

You will recall that we established two foundational premises that need to be communicated during the funeral. The first is that God is present; the second is that Jesus is alive. In this chapter, we must come back to them, review them, and apply them. If we lose this theme, then it will not make any difference as to the choices regarding the funeral service. To drift from them may pave the way to having a "celebration of life," but we will fail to assist the saints to handle time, and we will not prepare the sinners for eternity.

The Presence of God

> God *is* our refuge and strength, a very present help in trouble.
> Therefore will not we fear, though the earth be removed, and
> though the mountains be carried into the midst of the sea;
> *Though* the waters thereof roar *and* be troubled, *though* the
> mountains shake with the swelling thereof. Selah. (Ps. 46:1-3)

When describing all the calamities they had experienced on their way from Canaan to Egypt, Joseph's brothers used the word "trouble."[1] Here the psalmist uses the word to speak of his distress, trouble, affliction, and anguish.[2] From the context, the trouble of the writer's circumstances included danger, weakness, and fear, and his world had been "rocked." This is the world of the bereaved. The family's world has been shaken to the core. You must address the needs of these troubled hearts. What better way to help than to lead them to the God Who is their "refuge and strength"? What better way to help them navigate through the difficult weeks and months ahead than by reminding them that the God Who prepared them for eternity is the same God Who is "a very present help" in their distress? For a few minutes during the funeral service, all of time is put on hold, and you have the opportunity to comfort them by focusing their attention on the God Who is there. Note the end of verse 3 and the word "Selah." It is a musical term that indicates a cessation of movement and a time to think about what was just sung. "God is your refuge and strength. He is the God Who is here right now; He is the help, the aid, you desperately need. Think about it!"

The Resurrection of Christ

> Blessed *be* the God and Father of our Lord Jesus Christ, which according to his abundant mercy hath begotten us again unto a lively hope by the resurrection of Jesus Christ from the dead, To an inheritance incorruptible, and undefiled, and that fadeth not away, reserved in heaven for you, Who are kept by the power of God through faith unto salvation ready to be revealed in the last time. (1 Pet. 1:3–5)

Peter is writing to those who are experiencing many and difficult trials which are testing their faith. Your hearers are walking through a difficult trial as well, and it is testing their faith. What hope can you offer them? The resurrection of Christ is the only hope you can offer! Through the death, burial, and resurrection of Jesus, they can see the abundant mercy of God and be given an inheritance that will stand the test of time and eternity. Only through faith in the resurrected Christ can they face their own mortality. Do not view the funeral as taking advantage of the situation but perhaps as the one opportunity when you as "a dying man to dying men"[3] points to the One Who is the Living Water, the Bread of Life, the Resurrection and the Life—their only Hope!

"Among all the problems of the parish minister few are more baffling than those that concern funerals."[4] The following points in this chapter are designed to address those areas that you will face and that may seem daunting at the moment. One of the first opportunities I had to preach after entering the ministry as an assistant pastor tested my confidence and whether I was really ready to minister to God's people in this way. The senior pastor and my mentor, Richard Pettitt, quoted the following to me: "If any man speak, *let him speak* as the oracles of God; if any man minister, *let him do it* as of the ability which God giveth: that God in all things may be glorified through Jesus Christ, to whom be praise and dominion for ever and ever. Amen" (1 Pet. 4:11). And then he said, "On that night you preach, you are God's man with God's message for His people. Communicate the message God gives you with boldness and with the ability God gives you. It is not about you; it is about glorifying the Lord Jesus Christ, and God will enable you to fulfill this task." Timothy, what was true for me then is true for you now, and whether the funeral is tomorrow or a few days from now, look to God for help, and He will give it to you!

Current Trends

The very word *trends* indicates change, and we live in a world where changes can take place rapidly. For years we have seen the distancing of the living from the dead. One of the ways this has been accomplished is by the "celebration of life." This is not to say there should not be reflection on all the good the individual accomplished and the wonderful times the family had together; surely that is the joy of knowing and loving someone. But the pendulum can be swung so far that there is the ignoring of the fact that the loved one died and that those left behind must deal with the pain and separation. It is similar to the Puritan approach I wrote of earlier.

Other trends include death midwifery. It is the service of a paid individual to walk the family through caring for the deceased much in the way our great grandparents would have done, that is, without the services of a funeral director. Another is interactive headstones, which include a QR code so with a smartphone, a person can read about the one buried there. Cremains for many years have been scattered on the sea, but now you can pay for the cremains to be carried aloft high above the earth. When the urn reaches the right altitude, the ashes are released into the sky. There are also "green" burials using recycled wood or biodegradable products, so without the use of a vault, the body decomposes and becomes part of the earth. It has become more popular to have the funeral services centered around a theme, for example, the deceased's favorite film or activity. Whether traditional, a home funeral, or a thematic funeral, webcasting services are also offered for those not able to come because of time, distance, or cost.[5]

For some families, the size of the funeral service is controlled by having what is called a "mini-funeral." An invitation-only funeral is given for a close circle of family and friends.[6] There are also those who opt out of having a funeral or memorial service and have only what could be termed a wake. Family and friends are invited to a meeting place, where a spokesperson thanks those attending for the part they had in their loved one's life, and then they spend the rest of the time sharing stories and thoughts regarding the deceased.

I am not suggesting that these trends are antibiblical or wrong, but our Lord did not gather the family and friends of Lazarus to have them share memories of their brother and friend. He confronted their blindness to the presence of God and their ignorance of the power of the resurrection.[7] While celebrating the life of their loved one, you must point the family to the God Who is there and the hope of the resurrection.

The Funeral Service

Whether the aforementioned trends are followed or the family has asked you to perform a more or less traditional service, this chapter will help you communicate the dual theme of the presence of God and the resurrection of Christ. The presence and promise of God are communicated through the music, Scripture readings, poetic readings, testimonies, sermon, and even obituary. You have been stockpiling resources for years, and even yesterday, when you met with the family, you collected ideas and anecdotes you will use to personalize the service. The family desperately needs a messenger who knows God personally, but they greatly want someone who knew their loved one personally. God will use your familiar relationship with the deceased to open the hearts of the mourners and prepare them to receive the truths of the presence and promise of God.

Music

Music is the language of the heart. The Apostle Paul taught the Ephesians' and Colossians' churches to admonish one another by being filled with the Spirit and the Word so they could speak to each other "in psalms and hymns and spiritual songs, singing and making melody in (their) heart(s) to the Lord."[8] Funeral services with music can minister to the grieving heart very quickly. One of my sons, for a high school science fair project, discovered that different genres of music had a direct effect on the listener's blood pressure—some kinds raised it, others lowered it. Well-chosen music as a prelude to the service can quiet and prepare the hearts of the family for the truths they will hear. Familiar and favorite songs can bring comfort to those who are grieving. Hymns that speak of the presence of

God in trials can help the widow who is overwhelmed with loneliness. Songs that sing of the risen Savior and the glories of heaven can give the family hope. Music is a part of our worship, our play, our time to relax, our time to celebrate, and our time to mourn.[9]

"Sweet Beulah Land" is hymn 776 in our church's hymnal (my favorite hymn!) and always brings a sense of comfort and joy. "I'm kind of homesick for a country to which I've never been before. No sad goodbyes will there be spoken for time won't matter anymore."[10] In 1984, a wonderful man of God, active in our church and community, died due to injuries in an accident. Hundreds came to his funeral, and we were all comforted by the song sung by family friends titled "Finally Home":

> When engulfed by the terror of tempestuous sea unknown
> waves before you roll. At the end of doubt and peril is eternity.
> Though fear and conflict seize your soul. But just think of
> stepping on shore and finding it heaven of touching a hand and
> finding it God's of breathing new air and finding it celestial of
> waking up in glory and finding it home.[11]

Instrumental music, congregational singing, solos, small groups, or even a choir—music will minister to the hearts of the grieving. You will discover during your initial interview with the family the names of songs, requested musicians, and if congregational singing will be appreciated. As soon as possible, you need to contact those who will be involved. Recorded music is typically provided by the family and given to the director if the service is held at the funeral home. The director will have access to many recordings. If the service is to be held at the church, arrangements will need to be made with musicians and accompanists, instruments will need to be reserved, and perhaps a sound technician's time will need to be scheduled. This can be a lot of work, but good, godly, and well-performed music will bring glory to the Lord and comfort to all who attend.

The Obituary

What do we do with that? Based on the information gleaned from the family, the funeral director will write up a notice of the person's death. It will include the dates of birth and death and parents' names, along with other names of family living and deceased. As mentioned earlier, for newspaper use, it is best to keep it as brief as possible, but for the funeral service, it can be expanded with information regarding the deceased's education, employment, interests, and accomplishments. Most of the time, you will hear it read verbatim. Do not do this! This is a wonderful tool for you to bring a more personal approach to the presentation of the basic biographical facts. By the time you have finished rewriting, it will be more like a eulogy. Whether you have never met the individual or known him for a lifetime, the family and friends will appreciate you bringing a personal touch to an all-too-often sterile approach to just the facts. A couple of examples will help you understand what I mean.

Charles B. Boring

What was happening in 1934? FDR was in his first term as president of the United States. Clark Gable, Shirley Temple, and Gene Autrey, along with Laurel and Hardy, were starring in motion pictures. La Guardia was mayor of NYC. Dizzy Dean and his brother Paul pitched their way to winning the World Series for the St. Louis Cardinals. And Henry "Hank" Aaron, who broke Babe Ruth's homerun record, was born. All important people in the life of our beloved America, but whom we have never met. But, someone else was born in November of that year—someone you and I have had the privilege of knowing and loving.

Charles Benjamin Boring was born November 4, 1934, in a house on Welsh Hills Road and entered the presence of God this past Tuesday morning, November 9, from that same home. His parents were Fredrick and Bessie (Furbee) Boring.

Ben was a member of Bible Baptist Church since the year it began in 1961. He was an active member of the American Legion Post 398 of Granville, Licking County Veterans Alliance, and served as a warrant officer in the National Guard. From the pictures out in the foyer, you can tell he enjoyed bowling, loved his family, and enjoyed traveling. And there are not too many of us here who haven't enjoyed the fruit of his labor in the garden and the kitchen.

He was married to Margie Ann Dawson on March 10, 1956, in Richmond, Indiana. She, along with their children, continues to live in our community: three sons, Fred, Paul, and Dan; three daughters, Barbara, Lydia, and Rachel; three sisters, Marge Eikleberry, Harriet Bucklew, and Joyce Watson; and fifteen grandchildren.

Charles Benjamin Boring was born again into the family of God when he was a young man. He shared part of that wonderful experience with the family just a few days ago, saying he trusted Christ as his Savior, while attending the funeral of his father's friend. Later that day, he said, "Let me tell you the rest of the story . . . ," but was unable to finish it. It seems we'll have to wait until after we see Jesus in glory for Ben to fill us in.

Carolyn Sue Ross

Carolyn Sue (White) Ross, 68, of Granville, went to be with the Lord on August 28, 2013. She was born September 22, 1944, in Morgan County to the late Coral C. White and Bertha Louise (O'Neal) White Buckley.

LCAP employed Carolyn as a home health aide, where she was loved and appreciated by all. She was also very active at Bible Baptist Church in Newark.

Carolyn was a devoted daughter, wife, grandmother, great grandmother, sister, sister-in-law, aunt, great aunt, and friend. Carolyn greatly enjoyed the time she was able to spend with cherished loved ones and friends. She was often referred to as "the glue that held the family together." She loved baking, taking pictures, and serving to the needs of others.

Surviving is her husband of 48 years, Larry Lee Ross; sisters, Betty and Mary; brothers, Robert, Ronald, William, and Thomas White; grandchildren, Jeremy, Ashley, and Coral; and seven great grandchildren. In addition to her parents, she was preceded in death by her son David.

Scripture Reading

The Apostle Paul told his Timothy to "give attendance to reading."[12] From Nehemiah to Timothy, when the Bible speaks of reading, it is referring to the public reading of the Scriptures.[13] Reading and contemplating the Word of God gives hope and comfort. Psalm 119 is dedicated to the Word. In it, the psalmist declared that God caused him to hope when he heard the Word (verse 49). According to God's Word, he found comfort in God's merciful kindness (verse 76). He fainted for God's salvation but found hope in His Word (verse 81). He testified that God was his hiding place and shield and that he experienced hope in His Word (verse 114). There is great value in simply reading the Word of God in the funeral service.

Now, what shall we read? I will give you a suggested list in the resource chapter. From it, you can choose those passages that have been a help and comfort to the family over the past few days or the length of their loved one's illness. Perhaps you have discovered a favorite passage of the deceased, and communicating that just before you read it is just one more way to personalize the service. You will want to avoid long passages because you will lose people's attention. Perhaps since some of the "popular" passages are six verses, you might use that as a guide, for example, Psalm 23:1-6 and John 14:1-6.

Family Participation

Often the family will want to participate in the service or celebration. They may also have friends they would like to give a few minutes. Family and friends will certainly make the service personal; however, there are dangers associated with this. Desire does not equal ability, and it can be uncomfortable as someone struggles to communicate. Others will be overcome with emotion and not sure if they should continue. Then there are those who are either looking for their moment to lay out issues they had with the deceased or simply do not know when to stop. These dangers can be exacerbated if the opportunity is given with an invitation to anyone who has something he or she would like to share. It is, in my opinion, best to have two or three individuals designated to speak on behalf of the family and to give them a few simple instructions regarding where to stand and a suggested time constraint. If the family requests opening this to all who are present, you will want to control this time by keeping it moving and finally making a decision to close it off.

There could be a discussion with the family regarding paying the participants. In the funerals I have officiated, it is typically not done. I am aware that some churches expect their organist and other musicians to be compensated, but often those participating are either part of the family, friends, or associated with the church, and out of love for the individual, they will freely offer their time. An exception to this might be if someone has been specially requested and comes from a long distance. It would seem wise to care for their expenses. This would be the responsibility of the family and should be communicated to them early in the planning.

Organization Participation

The departed may have belonged to organizations that the family desires to be a part of the funeral services. Lodges have their rites that are to be performed on behalf of the deceased. These can be done the night before, for example, after the family visitation. They can also be done just before the funeral service itself. It is wise to have the lodge rites done first, and it is my experience they will appreciate it, so that afterward they can leave. Only lodge members who are close friends of the family will want to stay for the service.

If the individual was a veteran, the family might request that a veterans' organization, for example, Veterans Alliance, honor his or her service. If the veteran was on active duty, then you can expect that representatives from his or her unit will want to perform this service. As with the lodge, this may be performed as the service begins, or they may meet you at the cemetery and precede the graveside service. Services they provide include guards at attention as the body arrives at the cemetery and is moved from the hearse to the gravesite. When family and friends are seated at the funeral or standing near the gravesite, the honor guard will present the colors in the veteran's honor; a rifle squad will fire three volleys; "Taps" will be played; and the American flag draped on the casket will be folded and presented to the designated recipient. Then the honor guard will be dismissed, and the funeral or graveside service will continue. The funeral home will typically provide the flag and contact the veterans' organization to make these arrangements. Let me make one final comment on this: if the honor guard is waiting for the funeral procession at the cemetery, do all you can to make sure they are not waiting longer than expected. They are providing a free service, and their time should be respected.

The Funeral Sermon

There are trends that diminish the importance of the funeral sermon, but Timothy, take great care in the preparation and delivery of the message.[14] The saints are expecting a message of comfort from their spiritual leader. Their world has been shattered by this unnatural event, and they need to hear that God has not abandoned them. The unsaved are in desperate straits with their souls hanging between heaven and hell. As God's messenger, they need to hear from you the Gospel, and they may never be more open to the truth than they are on this day, when they are face-to-face with death.

If you have taken care to personalize the rest of the service, you can now direct your attention to the living, for "the lot of the deceased will not be affected by it."[15] The message must be clearly presented. This is not a time to impress people with your education and ability to communicate deep theology. You will want to present a simple, straightforward message. To continue with our theme, Timothy, direct them to Scriptures that declare in no uncertain terms that God is present and that the resurrection of Christ is more powerful than death and the grave.

Generally, funeral services are less than an hour, sometimes only a half hour, if there is little family participation or vocal music. The funeral sermon then should be no longer than fifteen minutes for a half hour and twenty minutes for a service that is forty-five minutes to an hour in length. This being the case, your sermon must move from its introduction into the body of the message rather quickly. Years ago, I was a member of Toastmasters International—an excellent organization to learn public speaking skills. They instructed us that the introduction should be no more than 10 percent of the speech, and likewise the conclusion. I have found this very helpful in forcing me to "set the stage and get to the point" within two minutes and then close in the same time.[16] As in the case of the hospital visit, better for them to wish you had spoken longer than to wish you were done.

The funeral sermon should be designed and delivered in a way that brings comfort to those who are morning and hope for the hopeless.[17] The Apostle Paul makes it clear that even the children of God experience grief, but not in the same way as those who have no hope.[18] He also states that the unsaved are without Christ, without God, and without hope.[19] You must minister to both, for most certainly it would be unusual for only the saved or the lost to be present. However, you can be sure that the Word of God can meet the needs of both. For you to address the grief of the believer, you will point them to why they have hope—the living God who is present. For you to speak to the one without hope about the One who gives hope will give comfort to the believer—the crucified and now resurrected Savior.

It will be to your advantage if you anticipate that one day you will perform a funeral. Whether in a small congregation or a large one, it is more likely your first service besides the stated worship services of the church will be a funeral rather than a wedding. In a year's time, you will have preached at the very least 50 sermons and perhaps as many as 150. Take note of those messages that would be appropriate for a funeral and file them as such. You will no doubt discover as well that your quiet times with the Lord generate thoughts that can later be developed into messages of comfort and hope. Consider the following circumstances and elements of the message, and I believe it will help you to choose your text.

Funerals are usually not services you can schedule. Your message will be no longer than fifteen to twenty minutes. The bereaved often have a difficult time processing their thoughts. It is likely you will have children as well as adults present. Your listeners will include those who are spiritually mature to babes in Christ or carnal Christians and the lost. For all of these reasons, the funeral sermon is not the place for a complicated text or a theological treatise. You should choose a text familiar to you and that may also be familiar to the mourners. Your text should be brief—just a few verses or perhaps even one. If you choose a longer narrative to preach, you will do well to relate it in story form and then read just the verses you will develop. In the bibliography, you will find books that list possible texts for a variety of occasions: a child, the elderly, suicide, and so on. I am not opposed to this, but I have discovered that a text that addresses comfort for the saved and hope for the lost can be delivered in a way to meet the diverse losses you will encounter. In "Resources" at the end of this book, you will find simple outlines that will get you started in your preparation.

Whether you choose a text from the Old Testament or the New, whether a narrative, a psalm, or a didactic passage, for you to communicate comfort for the saved and hope for the lost, you must declare the presence of God and the Gospel of Christ. You do not have to "get in their face" with the truth, but neither should you dance around the facts of death, grief, and eternity—they are already thinking about these. Please, O Timothy, do not just talk about the Gospel, proclaim it! Proclaim clearly that Christ died for our sins according the Scriptures and three days later was raised again according to the Scriptures for our justification.[20]

To demonstrate the preceding discussion, consider the following message and how you might revise it to make it your own.

Sermon Title: Hope for a Troubled Heart
Sermon Text: John 14:1–6

Introduction

1. Separation is painful, and it seems like it will last forever. At times it seems unreal, and next time we walk through the living room, our loved one will be sitting there—waiting for us. But they're not, and so we wonder, "Will I ever see them again?"
2. Jesus spoke of this pain in John 14.
3. It will be helpful to understand the context in which He said these words. It is just a few hours before the cross, and He tells His disciples . . .
    a. "I'm going to be lifted up" on a cross, i.e., I'm going to die.
    b. "One of you will betray me."

- c. To Peter, He said, "Before morning comes, you'll deny you know me three times."
- d. And He tells them, "Where I'm going you cannot come now, but you will follow me later."
4. With those devastating words, Jesus continues with John 14:1-6 (read).

I. HOPE FOR A TROUBLED HEART, v. 1
   a. With Jesus' prophecy of death, betrayal, denial, and abandonment, whose heart wouldn't be troubled?
   b. We live in a world that on the one hand has many wonderful surprises and joys—forty-eight years of love between a man and a woman, eight children, and rewarding work.
   c. On the other hand, there is pain and suffering and disappointments.
   d. In the middle of all these things, Jesus offers us hope; hope that begins with faith, belief.
   e. Belief in Someone Who transcends our grief and sorrows. Someone Who has faced all the pains and sorrows of death, betrayal, denial, and abandonment.
   f. Someone who has promised never to abandon us!
   g. That Someone is Jesus Christ, and because He is God, because He's alive, we have hope.

II. HOME FOR A DOUBTING HEART, vv. 2-3
   a. When we are facing death square in the face, our faith is tested. All of a sudden, we feel very insecure and vulnerable.
   b. It was then that Jesus told His disciples, His friends (for that is what He called them), that He was going away to build them a mansion.
   c. Often we read and hear of homes costing millions of dollars, thought to be permanent dwellings, quickly disappearing in a mudslide or a tsunami or a tornado.
   d. It is when our hearts are filled with doubts that Jesus comes along and tells us, "I'm building for you a home in heaven that cannot be destroyed."
   e. Along with the promise of a home in heaven, there is the promise that Jesus is coming for those who have believed in Him.
   f. Faith in God—faith in the Lord Jesus Christ—takes away the doubts that fill our hearts when trouble is around.

III. HELP FOR THE SEARCHING HEART, vv. 4-6

    a. In response to Jesus' statement, Thomas stated the searching question that's on all our minds.
    b. "How can we know the way? How can we know we will spend eternity in a place called heaven?"
    c. Jesus offers the direction we need; He gives us the help we need to satisfy the searching heart.
    d. In verse 6, Jesus tells us in terms that everyone can understand. The way to heaven is not something we do; it's not the result of a perfect or religious life. The way to heaven is a person.
    e. Jesus Himself is the way, the truth, and the life because He alone paid the price of our sin on the cross. He alone "was delivered for our offenses, and was raised again for our justification."
    f. He alone is the Hope for a troubled heart. He alone is building a Home for the doubting heart. He alone is the Help you need to satisfy the longing of a searching heart.

Conclusion

1. Jesus came to live, then die for your sins and mine, and then to have victory over death and the grave.
2. By faith, when we accept Christ as our personal Savior, He gives us . . .
   a. Hope for a troubled heart;
   b. Home for a doubting heart;
   c. Help for a searching heart.
3. I know your hearts are troubled. Some of you may be struggling with doubts. But I'm here to tell you that there is a God in heaven and He will give you the help you need if you just reach out to Him.

One final thought on the message: I want to encourage you to write it out word for word. Your time is limited; therefore your message must be clear, concise, and to the point. As you review the text, the outline, the explanation, and the illustrations, you can evaluate before you ever speak a word that its purpose will be fulfilled.

Prayer

Since our goal is to communicate the presence of God, you will want to pray during the funeral service. It seems natural to pray near the beginning and then to close the service. Prayer at the beginning could include the following: thanking God for His presence; thanking Him for the loved one's life and service; asking God's blessing on the service, that is, the music, His Word, and so on. The funeral director will instruct you that he will dismiss the mourners when you conclude the service. If you inform him that the last thing you will do is pray, it will help him to be prepared. When it comes to the benediction, some pastors have a memorized passage or statement that they will quote. I prefer not an impromptu prayer but a planned time for praying for the family, perhaps his wife and/or children by name. You can pray for God's comfort and love to surround them and wisdom for the future. This is a very personal prayer for the family. After you pray, make your way to the immediate family members who are seated near the front, offer to take their hands, express your condolences, and promise your continued prayer for them in the days ahead.

Dismissal

If there is a casket and a graveside service scheduled, after you have comforted the family, stand within proximity of the head of the casket while people are dismissed. Do not hover too close to the casket, for some will want to come and pay their final respects to the family and view the body one last time. Where you stand communicates, "I am here for you, if you need someone, and I will not leave your beloved's body alone until he or she is laid to rest at the cemetery."

If it has been an open casket during the service, the funeral director will dismiss the friends and family to close it up. You are there just to observe, though a time or two I have assisted in some small way, for example, by moving flowers or chairs to make exit by the pallbearers possible. Having secured the casket, the director will invite the pallbearers to carry the casket to the hearse. You will walk before them and stand to the side of the hearse until the casket is secured inside. It is at this time you will either sit on the passenger side of the hearse or make your way to your own vehicle. This travel arrangement will be made before the funeral service begins, for upon your arrival at the funeral home, you will be asked whether you will be driving yourself to the cemetery or riding in the hearse. I want to encourage you if at all possible to ride in the hearse for several reasons. This communicates to the family your care for the loved one, but it is also a wonderful time to get better acquainted with the director or the designated driver. Over a period of years, you will develop a relationship with the funeral personnel, and they have spiritual needs as well. It is possible they have no more hope of heaven than those to whom you spoke during the service. While you are traveling to the cemetery for the graveside service, you are God's messenger for that person, too.

Final Details

Not everyone is a detail person, so a final word on the funeral seems appropriate. My grandparents were parents of the Greatest Generation, so good manners meant something else to them than it might to others. To go to the grocery store meant Grandpa put on a clean dress shirt and a tie and his best dress hat. Grandma put on one of her better dresses and made sure the grandkids were clean and presentable. Be aware of your local culture and that of your church. Appropriate dress at the visitation time might be business casual. For the funeral, you will always be acceptable if you wear business dress.[21] For our community, that means a suit and a tie—preferably a dark suit. I have a black suit that I save for weddings and funerals, and it is always in style. Make sure yours is clean and pressed. Drop a few breath mints in your pocket, and use them! Arrive at the funeral home or whatever venue is being used at least thirty minutes ahead of time. As my military friends say, "Better to be two hours early than two minutes late!" This will ease the mind of the family that you will be on time. Bring copies of the order of service for all participants, and speak briefly to each of them to make sure all are ready. It is embarrassing and unnecessary to be waiting for a participant in the service only to discover that she has opted out. You will especially take some time with the funeral director so that he and you can work together. Typically, a funeral home will have a place for you to wait for the start of the service. Arriving early will give you time to take advantage of this by reviewing the service order one more time, making sure of the first words you will be speak, praying, and relaxing. If you are involved in a law enforcement funeral, a police department's chaplain will be able to guide you in the protocol for an officer's funeral. If the officer was killed on duty, the police department will see it as their duty to be heavily involved in, if not lead, the services. Welcome their part in it, for in this case, no doubt dozens, if not hundreds, of officers from the state and the country will come to honor their brother or sister. Without their help or lead, it will be overwhelming for you, the family, and your congregation.[22]

Recently, I was waiting at a cemetery for the family to arrive and spent a few minutes reading the words on the grave markers. Two of them were for young men in their thirties when they died. One stated that no one should weep for him, for he was not there. I thought this was good, but then as I read further, it said he was in the winds of the sky and the stars above. How very sad. The other admonished the reader not to mourn the loss of him, as he was right here with them and would never leave them. Perhaps someone longed to comfort families and friends when they visited the graves, but the sentiments could not be further from the truth. During a funeral or memorial service, you may not be able to undo a lifetime of unfortunate theology or philosophy, but throughout the hour you spend with the family and friends, you can point them to the God Who is ever present and to that blessed hope and the glorious appearing of the Great God and our risen Savior Jesus Christ.[23] By the grace of God, the power of His Word, and the ministry of the Holy Spirit, they will experience comfort in their grief and hope for their tomorrows.

CHAPTER SEVEN

THE GRAVESIDE SERVICE
A Necessary Parting

"So death for the Christian is at once deadly serious and profoundly awe-inspiring. It is not God's last word. We wait for the Resurrection."[1] Any hope you associate with the last enemy can only be realized in light of the final victory.

> Death is swallowed up in victory. O death, where *is* thy sting? O grave, where *is* thy victory? The sting of death *is* sin; and the strength of sin *is* the law. But thanks *be* to God, which giveth us the victory through our Lord Jesus Christ.[2]

For nearly every graveside service or interment, while riding to the cemetery, I am turning to this passage. Only by the revelation of God can we offer any hope beyond the grave—we have never been there, but He is there. This very same hope was held by Job at least two thousand years before Paul.

> For I know that my redeemer liveth, and that he shall stand at the latter day upon the earth: And though after my skin worms destroy this body, yet in my flesh shall I see God: Whom I shall see for myself, and mine eyes shall behold, and not another; though my reins be consumed within me. (Job 19:25-27)

By the time family and friends drive away from the cemetery, this truth ought to have been fully planted in their hearts and ringing in their ears. That being the case, you will focus your attention on the resurrection of Christ and the resurrection of mankind. This can be of great comfort to the believers, but we cannot offer the same to the lost. You will remember there are two resurrections—not just two events but two kinds of resurrection.

> Marvel not at this: for the hour is coming, in the which all that are in the graves shall hear his voice, And shall come forth; they that have done good, unto the resurrection of life; and they that have done evil, unto the resurrection of damnation. (John 5:28-29)

This is not a text on theology, but for you to confidently communicate the hope of the resurrection, I suggest you review several trusted volumes on man and the resurrection. For clarification, let me remind you that at death, the body and soul (and spirit) separate. The soul enters into eternity to be with Christ[3] or await judgment in hell.[4] We honor the deceased by caring for his body, and then we wait for the resurrection. The resurrection of life is for those who are righteous "or they who by their good works 'show' that they are the friends of Christ"[5] and dressed in His righteousness.[6] The resurrection of damnation is reserved for those who are condemned by the righteous Judge to everlasting judgment.[7]

Just as there are two resurrections, there are two kinds of individuals who will come to the cemetery for the committal service.[8] There will be the believers in various stages of maturity. There will no doubt also be unbelievers. Because of the power of the Word of God, the work of the Holy Spirit, and the marvelous gift of language, the Lord can use you to minister to each one on some level. What can you expect, and what is expected of you?

In most of the funerals you will participate in, since you are riding in the hearse, you will be in the lead car. In Ohio, whenever the lead car enters an intersection, whether by a green light or proceeding after a stop sign, all the other cars may follow regardless of the lights or signs, as long as they can do so safely.[9] The funeral director will, of course, be acquainted with the specific laws in your state. Often upon arriving at the cemetery, the vehicles will be directed to the burial plot by the caretakers, and another individual, sometimes the worker from the vault company, will let the driver know where to stop. Fifteen to twenty years ago, I was still being instructed by the driver to wait in the car until he was ready to call for the pallbearers, and then he would open the door for me. Those days are past around here. If the weather is tolerable, you can immediately exit the hearse and stand eight to ten feet to the rear of the vehicle. In inclement or frigid weather, you will want to wait until the pallbearers have been called. If the funeral director has not pointed out the path to the gravesite, you should use this time to determine the best route. Remember that six pallbearers and a heavy casket along with the family and friends will be following you, so walk at an easy pace so as not to get too far from them or hinder their progress.

When you approach the gravesite, typically the vault employee will indicate where the head of the casket will be placed. Stay out of the way of the pallbearers, but as soon as their work is completed, stand near the head and under the tent if one is provided. Be sure of your footing, for you are near a hole that may be up to six feet deep. As to why we stand at the head rather than the feet, I can only assume it is simply tradition. The mourners will be seated and standing to the side of the coffin. If for some reason they will be standing at one end, typically you will be at the feet and the family at the head. Wait quietly in position until the director indicates you may begin, that is, after the family and friends have all arrived and taken a position as close as possible.

Unless you have been blessed with a naturally loud voice, you will need to make an extra effort to project your words to the ones farthest away. Other challenges to being heard will include traffic noise on a nearby road, older people with hearing difficulties, and children who are easily distracted. Let me also suggest that you not take any notes with you, just your Bible. A small Bible or New Testament is best due to possible windy conditions, and you can control the pages better. Dare I add this? Have you remembered your glasses? Have you remembered to silence your cell phone or leave it in the hearse? One frigid January, as I took my warm glasses out of my pocket and put them on, the change in temperature affected the frames, and the lenses fell to the ground! Fortunately, the director offered me his so I could read, and, of course, we have all been in a service where someone's cell phone rings. Do not let it be yours!

If the family has selected to recognize the deceased's military service at the cemetery rather than at the funeral home or church, you will want to plan for this to take place first. The honor guard has been at the cemetery at least an hour before you arrived and had already begun to honor him or her by standing at attention when the hearse arrived and when the casket was transferred from the hearse to the gravesite. As described in the previous chapter, they will honor their fallen comrade by firing three volleys, playing "Taps," and folding and presenting the American flag, and then they will be dismissed. Though the entire committal service is normally less than ten minutes in length, the family may have also requested that others besides you participate. I highly recommend you ask them to go first so that you can have the final word. Yes, I officiated at funerals where I was not the last to speak, and let me just say, it did not end well.

Your part of the committal will traditionally include the following: Scripture reading with a brief comment, then some ministers like to give a well-known statement taken from Ecclesiastes 12:7, "Then shall the dust return to the earth as it was: and the spirit shall return unto God who gave it," that is, "Earth to earth, ashes to ashes, dust to dust," followed by prayer.[10] Though a respectful way to end the services, I find this too impersonal, and it seems to communicate that the depositing of the body in the grave is the final word. It also leaves a lot of unanswered questions in the minds of the children and the biblically uninformed who may be present. It has been stated and confirmed by multiple authors that the committal service should be brief, that is, less than ten minutes—some would say five to six minutes.[11] If weather permits, the services I lead are closer to ten minutes. In the following pages, I have re-created what I say and do at the graveside. It is not too much different than what I have described earlier, but it takes into account my premise, the two truths that need to be emphasized throughout the day—the presence of God and the resurrection of Christ with a personal touch.

My Graveside Service

On behalf of the family, thank you for being with us this afternoon. When we come to the cemetery, it can be overwhelming, because it seems so final. It is comforting to the family to have you here. A moment ago, I did say, "It seems so final." The truth is a cemetery, this place right here, is only a temporary stopping point. Even the name *cemetery* communicates this, because the word simply means "a sleeping place." When Jesus spoke about a little girl and also His friend Lazarus after they had died, He said they had fallen asleep. That means, dear friends, there is more to come. It is called the Resurrection. Listen to what the Apostle Paul had to say about it. I am reading from 1 Corinthians chapter 15.

> *Now this I say, brethren, that flesh and blood cannot inherit the kingdom of God; neither doth corruption inherit incorruption. Behold, I shew you a mystery; We shall not all sleep, but we shall all be changed, In a moment, in the twinkling of an eye, at the last trump: for the trumpet shall sound, and the dead shall be raised incorruptible, and we shall be changed. For this*

corruptible must put on incorruption, and this mortal must put on immortality.

So when this corruptible shall have put on incorruption, and this mortal shall have put on immortality, then shall be brought to pass the saying that is written, Death is swallowed up in victory. O death, where is thy sting? O grave, where is thy victory? The sting of death is sin; and the strength of sin is the law. But thanks be to God, which giveth us the victory through our Lord Jesus Christ.

This body we have now is not fit for heaven. It must be changed. Unfortunately, that means we have to walk through the valley of the shadow of death. Today it is necessary for Brother Wilson to inherit a new body—one that is free from the pain that he experienced for so long. There is coming a day when his mortal body will be changed, in the twinkling of an eye. It will happen when that trumpet shall sound, and the dead shall be raised incorruptible. It is a marvelous truth; it is the blessed hope.

I remember standing where you stand right now. My mother had died, and my two brothers and I, a few hours after her funeral, were at her grave swapping memories. It was wonderful, but then it seemed like a dark cloud came over one of my brothers, and in anguish and pain, he cried out, "It's not fair. Why does it have to end like this? She never did anything wrong. I don't understand. Someone should write a book to help us." He was experiencing "the sting of death," and it was very painful.

Well, I have just read to you from that Book. It tells us that because of the resurrection of Christ and by your faith in Him Who died for you and rose again, when you come to this place, the sting is gone! You will grieve, but you do not have to grieve as those who have no hope. If you have not trusted Christ as your Savior, I urge you to come to Him today. If you have even one question about it, I will do my best to help you find the answer. Let's pray.

Precious Father, we thank you for the life of Brother Wilson. What a blessing he was to us all. Thank you, too, for his dear wife, Linda, and the children and their families. May this place generate wonderful memories from the past but also comforting hope for the future. Give the family wisdom for any decisions they will face. I pray, too, that they will sense Your presence in the days ahead. We ask all this in Jesus' name, our Savior, our risen Lord, and soon-coming King. Amen.

However you choose to conclude the service, perhaps with a closing prayer, make your way to the immediate family, who most often will be seated in front of you. Assure them of your prayers while shaking their hands. Your Bible speaks of a holy kiss, in this case, a holy handshake or a hug.[12] With their loved one gone, a human touch is very meaningful and appropriate at this time. This is typically the sign for the director to dismiss the family and friends and to direct them to their cars. As we will note in a moment, there may be a final good-bye through the release of a dove or balloons.

This service can be the most difficult for some. It is the final good-bye, which is what they have dreaded from the moment the news of the impending death was heard. They are leaving their friend, their spouse, their parent, perhaps a child, hovering over the cold dark earth, and who is strong enough to face this alone? Surely the presence of God and the hope of the resurrection bring comfort to the child of God at this time.

There are some variations to the committal service that are an attempt not only to "bring closure" but also to enable the mourners to have "a happy memory." Some funeral directors provide the service of releasing a dove at the conclusion of the service. Words spoken as the dove is released may be as follows: "Today we lay (name) to rest. Let us remember the peace and joy she brought to her friends and family, the love and understanding she gave so willingly, and generously, to all of you. This bird in flight symbolizes the end of her life on earth and the beginning of life with the Lord Jesus Christ."[13] It is certainly dramatic, and adults, of course, would comprehend the symbolism, but young children are so literal in their comprehension that they may miss the imagery. Other symbols of release used are helium balloon and butterflies.[14] The first time I saw helium balloons released, I was standing near my father's grave, and a family fifty yards or so away from me had the children release white balloons. It was a dramatic ending, and the children as well as the adults watched them for a long time as they disappeared. Again, though, I am afraid the symbolism of it all would have been lost to the young.

Do not be in a hurry to leave when the director dismisses the family. This is sometimes an opportunity for you to minister if but for a few moments to the bereaved. If the weather is nice and the family is close, they may stand around visiting for quite a while. There are times you may be able to minister to a family member, perhaps an estranged child, who is overcome with guilt and grief and who feels he just cannot leave his loved one. If the church is providing a meal after the service, you may have to encourage the family to carry on their visiting at that venue, so as not to make the workers wait and wonder. The funeral director, the vault company worker, and the caretakers will also be grateful, for they cannot complete their work until the family has left the cemetery. A dear friend of mine, we'll call him "Dr. Mike," told me he chooses to stay at the gravesite while the family drives away. He wants them, when they look back, to see him, their pastor, instead of an unattended casket and a mound of dirt.[15] What a treasured memory to give your flock.

Timothy, you might think that your work with the grieving family is concluded, but this whirlwind of activity that has taken place over the last three days is not the end. You will have opportunities to bring comfort to the family many times over the next few weeks and months, if not years. Chapters 9 and 10 will address an immediate need and the future occasions where you and the church family can come alongside to share in their sorrow and help them through the healing process to arrive at their "new norm." First, let us consider your close associate during these past days: the funeral director.

CHAPTER EIGHT

THE FUNERAL DIRECTOR
Co-laborer or Combatant?

> Our new Constitution is now established, and has an appearance that promises permanency; but in this world, nothing can be said to be certain, except death and taxes.
> —Benjamin Franklin, in a letter to Jean-Baptiste Leroy, 1789

With nearly three million deaths every year in the United States, in all likelihood, within the first year of your ministry, you will be called upon to officiate at a funeral.[1] When that happens, the first voice you will hear over the phone will often be that of a local funeral director. One of the fifty-five thousand in the United States will inform you of the name of the individual who has died and that the family is sitting in his office and has requested that you perform the service.[2] He (or she) is not a stranger to death. He is well trained and experienced in this field of caring for the dead.[3] He will arrange and care for the moving and preparation of the body. In accordance with the law, he will file death certificates and other legal documents. Most can provide emotional support to the bereaved.[4] Though you will find many who are believers in Christ, you will also discover that most will not cross over to take your responsibility of caring for the spiritual needs of the family. Unless you give him cause to do otherwise, he will respect your office, and you will do well to respect his place in the family's life. He is in fact a co-laborer with you.

Professional Co-laborers

The responsibility of caring for the dead has shifted over time. Early in American history, the family or perhaps a group of women had the responsibility of preparing the body for burial. The place for laying out the body has shifted as well. What was once done in the private home is now attended to in a professional funeral home.

The reasons why the care of the body for the viewing and burial has shifted over the years are more societal than legal. For the last 150 years, we have become a more mobile and affluent society. Our homes are often too small and not equipped for the care of the dead. We have also distanced ourselves from the dead, and so, enter the professional funeral director.

This person enables us to leave the care of the preparation of the body to be preserved for viewing days later, giving family members from great distances time to arrive. The funeral home also provides a facility large enough for family and friends to be received. The grieving family can concentrate on caring for the living family members and friends as well as their own emotional state. Certainly there are expenses associated with the professionals handling this, but for most of us, it is the preferable method. They are in fact better equipped to handle this end-of-life responsibility.[5]

Though it is legal in many states for the family to care for the dead, it can be presumed that since it took a long time to shift from the personal home to the professional, it will take an equally long time to shift back or at the least to become received as a viable option. Home funerals where the family chooses to care for the body of their loved one are growing in acceptance. The work of hospice care, enabling the family to keep their loved one at home rather than in an institution, has been a natural step toward this.

Funeral directors, sometimes called morticians or undertakers, have earned at least a two-year associate degree followed by a one- to three-year apprenticeship as a mortuary science technician. For their training, the American Board of Funeral Service Education accredits approximately fifty-five mortuary science programs. At these schools, they study anatomy, embalming practices, funeral customs, psychology, accounting, and public health laws. Nearly one-fourth of their training is spent in laboratory studies. After completing their education and apprenticeship, they must pass a state board examination. This includes written and oral testing as well as demonstrating proficiency of skills. Owing to the nature of their work, they must also be compassionate, sympathetic, and discreet. They would, of course, need to have physical strength as well as restorative skills to care for the moving and preparation of the body for viewing.[6]

Funeral directors enter this field because they see it as a calling. Some have grown up in their parents' business, but many men and women have had no prior connection to the field. Their work is filled with long hours, including weekends and holidays. On any given day, they must quickly transition from transportation to medical-like procedures to a businessperson and a counselor. In a small business, there will be long hours of waiting, then within twenty-four to seventy-two hours, they must pick up the body and have it ready for the funeral. Besides all the physical work, there will be phone calls to make (one to you!), forms to fill out, and arrangements for florists, pallbearers, visitation times, vault companies, and cemeteries, along with transportation. The average director will do this twice a week.[7] Larger funeral homes in metropolitan areas will have many more.[8] Their annual income for all this work ranges from $28,000 to $95,000, with a median of $51,600.[9] Timothy, their calling is not the same as yours, but you can see that for most of them, it is not a lucrative occupation when you consider all they will do for your families. It is a chosen vocation for them to help people in their time of need.

Shortly after you arrive at your new ministry, I want to encourage you to spend an hour with a local funeral director. If you ask your deacons, they will be able to tell you which funeral home or homes your congregation has used in the past. Whether in a metropolitan area or a rural setting, you will discover someone who has committed her life to caring for the dead and who will be more than happy to get acquainted with you and your ministry. Over the years, I have developed friendships with the directors in the cities I have served. It is not as strange as it may seem. They have families, belong to houses of worship, and are involved in the community in other ways besides their businesses. They have a sense of humor, too. Whatever morbid concept you have regarding their profession, they are as common as any other professionals you will meet—and they can be your mentors and friends. They are, in fact, your co-laborers, not combatants or competitors.

The View from the Hearse

Timothy, you can learn a lot from the one sitting in the driver's seat of the hearse. The nature of his service demands that he remain neutral regarding the spiritual views of his clients. He is attempting to meet the needs and desires of the families he serves. He values your input to the bereaved but needs for you to be flexible as well—not to forget your theology but to be willing to adapt to the family's wishes as much as possible. Here are some wonderful insights you will gain by asking questions and listening.[10]

You will find funeral homes in every region of our country. They are located in metropolitan areas, suburbs, villages, and rural locations. The visitation times and funeral services vary and are not predictable based on the South or the West or wherever you are located. In some places, 85 percent of the services are held in the funeral homes, and in other locations, only 25 percent. On average, half of them will be held in the funeral home, a quarter will be in a church or temple, 10 percent will be at the graveside, and 15 percent will have no service at all.[11]

Most of the time, the directors will not say anything to you regarding how you perform your duties, but if you ask her how you can help make her job easier or more effective or how the two of you can best work together for the benefit of the family, she will share with you some great insight. Think of your work, her work, and the family's wishes as a team effort. Often the family will have already met with the director and communicated where and when they would like the visitation time, the funeral, and, of course, the place of interment. Be assured that the director will have communicated to the family that all these decisions are tentative until you are brought into the discussion. Some families will invite you into the first discussion with the director, which can be helpful. Please note that this is not the time to design the actual service. The mortician has many details that must be acted upon, and this first meeting is for her work. Service plans come later.[12]

Before the visitation, sometimes called a viewing, it will be good, if at all possible, for you to be there when the family sees their loved one's body in the casket for the first time. It can be a very emotional time, as the reality of his death comes into full view. The directors have been trained for that moment, but how much better for their pastor to be there with them. On occasion you will find it important to be with the family during the visitation hours; however, when there is a steady flow of friends and family, your presence will not be needed. Just before you leave the funeral home is a good time to communicate once again with the director and, if possible, with the director who will be attending to the funeral service. You can go over the service order, the details of instruments needed, or the playing of CDs, as well as cues for the beginning and conclusion of the service.[13]

The ideas communicated in this chapter are partially mine, but most of them have come from the funeral directors who were gracious enough to take the time to help me. They are also very candid in revealing ways we as preachers hinder their work or bypass the desires and needs of the families. For example, when the director leaves a message on your answering machine, you need to call her directly and as soon as possible. Do not use the bereaved family as your messenger. The director must make confirmations with many parties, and the sooner she can do this, the better it will be for all.

The directors want us to be as flexible as possible. Contemporary funerals are often theme oriented to the pastimes of the deceased, for example, sports (football, golf) or sportsman (fishing, hunting). The director has attempted to meet this wish of the family, and for us to come in later and change it or squelch it altogether is not kind to anyone. If it is at your church, you will have more control over this, but at the funeral home, you are the director's guest. You will find this especially true when working with "nonchurch" families. The directors would have us know that when we stubbornly impose our traditions and agendas on the unsaved, as well as being judgmental toward the unchurched, we do more harm than good. Along with this, some directors communicated that the pastors made changes in the arrangements of the times, days, and locations without their input. This is just being disrespectful of others' time and work.

One director was concerned about the amount charged by the pastor for a half-hour service. We have already addressed this earlier in the book, that is, when the services are local, this is your opportunity to minister, even if not compensated. God will take care of you without you putting a price on your time. Out-of-town services are different in that I believe there can be the expectation that your expenses will be covered. Some final words from the directors include the following: be available to the family so that they do not have to go through the director to get to you; get involved in the family's life during these days and do your best to help them. When a family requests you to be concise or brief, adhere to their wishes. It is a turn off to religion to "overpreach." Also, the funeral directors want you to know they appreciate your involvement, your support, and your help.[14]

A Friend and Co-laborer

During a radio call-in program, though the callers did not list specifics, they communicated the perception that funeral directors are "rapacious, unctuous, willing to feign compassion for profit, ready to take advantage of people in their most vulnerable moments and eager to shill for unnecessary goods and services—in short . . . bottom feeders."[15] In more than forty years of ministry, I can think of two instances when I wondered about the actions of a funeral director and only one time when I was sure the director was not being honest. Timothy, I am afraid I can think of too many pastors who have struggled in the areas of ethics, compassion, and morality. You would do well to find a funeral director for a friend. He can be a great resource for you. When you add up his time in the classroom, the laboratory, and apprenticeships, his training is either equal to or surpasses the training most of us had when we entered the ministry. He may not be a believer, but he has committed himself and his business to function with high ethics in the areas of fraud, deceit, misrepresentation, intimidation, family wishes, and religion.[16]

A few years ago, we traveled back to a city where I had served for fifteen years for the visitation of an old friend who had died. It had been more than twenty years since I had last stepped into that funeral home. My wife and I were greeted by one of the directors whose family had served that community for several generations. I was not surprised when I recognized him; however, I was greatly surprised when he recognized me. We greeted one another as old friends. That impressed me with the fact that this man, this family business, was committed to the community, the families, and the churches they served.

Many times, the following verse is associated with Christ, and truly He is closer than a brother, but the primary application is to two people who have been brought together in the experiences of life. "A man that hath friends must shew himself friendly: and there is a friend that sticketh closer than a brother" (Prov. 18:24). There are two funeral homes in our community that our church families have used more than the others. The directors there are more than businesspeople; they are our friends, and they are co-laborers as we minister together to the ones who are walking through the most difficult times of their lives.

CHAPTER NINE

THE FUNERAL MEAL
Blessing or Burden?

Have you noticed that when someone dies, it is not very long before a neighbor shows up at the door with a covered dish, a pie, or a basket of fruit? Why is that? It seems that when people are at a loss as to what to say but feel they must do something, food is their answer. They are not far off from biblical truth in that response. Get your Bible and join me in Genesis 18. I will be there in a moment.

In your Bible, the word *heart* is used 876 times, and every time, it is speaking of the immaterial part of man. As you know, the essence of man is immaterial and material, and these parts are connected in such a way that one affects the other. When people are plunged into sorrow through the death of a loved one, their hearts are broken, and it affects them physically. Friends are hurting with them; they desperately want to comfort the bereaved, and the first thing that comes to mind is Grandma's famous recipe. They hurriedly whip it up, cover it up, and take it over to minister to the bereaved family and somehow comfort them.

We have all used the phrase *comfort food*. The modern use of the term dates to 1966, when someone coined it to speak of the ability of the right food to help with emotional stress.[1] When our stress is running high, or we are emotionally distraught, we sometimes turn to food that gives us a sense of well-being, a sense of belonging. The smell and the taste take us to a place mentally and emotionally where we feel safe, satisfied, rested, and comforted.

Are you in Genesis 18? Take a moment to read verses 1-8. Three visitors from heaven were walking toward Sodom and stopped to see the man of God. Hospitality during this time of history was at a whole different level than what we do. Abraham offered water to wash their feet, a shade tree to rest under, and bread to eat. They accepted his offer, and this ninety-nine-year-old man took off running! Abraham was concerned for their physical needs and their hearts. His anticipation of the meal that would be fixed is that it would "comfort" their hearts and strengthen them.

> Let a little water, I pray you, be fetched, and wash your feet,
> and rest yourselves under the tree: And I will fetch a morsel of
> bread, and **comfort** ye your hearts; after that ye shall pass on:
> for therefore are ye come to your servant. (Gen. 18:4–5)

The word *comfort* (סעד, sâ'ad) is used twelve times in the Old Testament. It means "to support, to refresh, to strengthen," and five times it is used of food. The others speak of the Lord's work in our lives.[2] If you want to comfort someone, then it is biblical to start cooking! We will see that it is very practical and appreciated by those who have been touched with sorrow.

Individuals, organizations, and employers associated with the deceased are often very quick to offer this gift; moreover, your church can come alongside the family in a huge way to meet the needs of the mourners. For example, it had been a long day. The family had risen early in the morning to take care of details that could not be done the day before, for example, picking up a relative from the airport or caring for things that were inadvertently forgotten—clothes needing washing or a run to the store to replace a dress that needed mending. Breakfast was a cup of coffee and a bagel, or perhaps they did not feel like they could eat. Then they arrived at the funeral home two hours before the service for a final visitation time. The service was forty-five minutes long. The ride to the cemetery and the graveside service was another hour. When all was said and done, as they made their way home, someone in the back seat said, "What's for supper?"

What a wonderful gift to the family to be able to say to that young voice in the back, "Son, the church has prepared a meal for us. Your cousins will be there, friends from church, and others who came today will also be there. Miss Vicki told me she fixed your favorite dessert. You'll be fine." Even before they arrive at the church, this young child who is hurting is also comforted. The meal after the services should be considered by your church a blessing to the part of the Body of Christ that is hurting, never a burden!

Consider all the other benefits to the family. After the funeral, there is an emotional release. People were tense thinking about how they would respond to friends who came to see them. Would they cry when the soloist sang Mom's favorite hymn? Grandpa felt like he must be strong for the rest of the family. There will be more days of crying and remembering, but as they walked away from the casket for the last time, a little bit of healing had taken place, and they sighed with relief. They were not before, but now they are hungry!

This day is a little bit of sweet and sour. They are grieving; their eyes hurt from crying; but today they see relatives whom they have not seen for years. It is wonderful! Notes at Christmas time are not enough for extended families, and weddings and funerals bring them together. While they sit around the table enjoying the banquet your church has provided, they are reconnecting with the relatives. The thought that it will only last for an hour or two has not crossed their minds. For the moment, they are fully engaged, learning what others have been up to and reminiscing about old times.

It is also a time for the church to serve their friends. The fellowship the workers enjoy while caring for the Body cannot be purchased online or at the Christian bookstore. These servants are often the ones who cannot sing, cannot teach, are not gifted in any other way, but they can cook, they can set up tables, fill the serving bowls, smile, and in a couple of hours, they can clean. It has been a long day for them as well, but they can go home tired and happy, satisfied for the opportunity to minister to hurting brothers and sisters. They will also remember how the grieving family stopped at the kitchen door to say over and over again, "Thank you!"

The Body of Christ is a marvelous gift from God, and it does not matter how large or how small your flock is—they can do this. How do you make it happen? Let me suggest a few steps to take and ways you can lead your church.

Point Man or Woman

I am convinced that whatever the Body of Christ needs, God has gifted someone in the church to fulfill that need. At our church, we have a very gifted woman to care for funeral dinners. She was the head cook at our local high school. She knows what and how to cook for large crowds, and she knows how to direct the work of others. Look around your church family, especially while you are enjoying a church dinner. Your Point Man is there; you just need to identify him or her.

Shortly after you hear from the family that a death has occurred, one of your phone calls will be to the Point Man. You do not have any details yet, but you have her standing ready, and she is already thinking.

Later you will call her again to tell her when the dinner is needed and approximately how many the family expects will be staying. From this information, she will determine how much food will be needed, what she will buy already prepared, for example, fried chicken, how many side dishes and desserts will be needed, as well as beverages that must be arranged. At the end of this chapter, you will find examples of menus and amounts to prepare based on the size of the group expected.

The Setup Crew

Having determined the day and approximate number coming, tables and chairs need to be set up in your fellowship hall or gym. Years ago, we thought round tables would be a good idea, so we purchased a dozen. We have since learned that they are not very conducive for visiting. You can see everyone, but it is difficult to speak to those across the table, who can be five feet away. You end up talking only to those beside you. It is better to get out those eight-foot tables and play with the different ways they can be arranged. End to end may look right, but you lose two seats on each table. You can easily seat ten. Make sure they are clean! Set out the trash cans and a place for used silverware, if needed, away from the food. Regardless of how many tables are to be set up, invite others to help. For example, if the funeral is on a Monday or Tuesday, the teenagers and their teacher can get the tables and chairs out after the Sunday morning or evening service. This engages them in a small way of serving others.

For a small group, that is, twenty-five to fifty, you can set up a single set of serving tables so you have two lines, one on either side. For fifty or more, you will want at least four serving lines, that is, two sets of serving tables. If you have a dessert table and a drink table separate from these lines, the dinner lines will move rapidly, assuring that the food is still hot. It may seem for some that the details I have added are unnecessary to include in this text, but having been at my share of church and funeral dinners, the preceding works well, and you can pass this on to your Point Man, if needed.

What about lining up the food? We include in our church budget money to order flowers for the funeral but also for a main dish and beverages. I have been to funerals where the church or a service organization to which the deceased belonged charged the family for the meal. Please do not do this! Get it in the budget. We try to accommodate the family's desires for this, but typically in our Midwest church, it turns out to be fried chicken or ham. There are families who request sandwiches, depending on the time of day or the plans they have for later. Having decided on the menu, our Point Man has a list of names of those in our church who have told her they want to help for funeral dinners. She has learned that certain people have specialty items they like to prepare. The others are asked to fill in where needed. Then there are singles and couples who have told her they are available for setup, serving, and cleanup, so she contacts them with the particulars.

During the meal, the kitchen crew tries to maintain a low profile to give the family privacy to visit with their family and friends; however, many times, they are asked to join them, so when the work is mostly done, they do. After the dinner, the crew boxes up the leftover food that can be used and sends it home with the family. This helps the family care for extended relatives who may be staying with them. Then the cleanup begins. We have been so blessed in this area because the church family has come to believe this meal is ministry, and it is. After all are gone, the only evidence that a meal was served that day is the aroma. Our Point Man said there was no need to mention her name, but without Veva, this ministry would just not be the same!

A Few More Details

Imagine the family, relatives, and friends coming from the cemetery to your church. They will not all arrive at the same time. Many have never been to your church, so they will be looking for the right door to enter. Those same younger souls who have been carrying dishes of food from the cars to the kitchen can now act as your greeters. They will welcome and direct them. Have them point out the coatracks, the restrooms, and the room set up for the meal. Some might even need to find a changing table. Children will love to guide the guests, so let them serve!

Speaking of children, remember to include on the menu a few things kids like to eat, for example, macaroni and cheese and chicken nuggets.[3] As for beverages for everyone, keep it simple. We used to go through a couple dozen liters of soda pop; however, now we seem to be living in a more health-conscious society, so coffee (decaffeinated) and bottled water are just fine. If you want something a little different, pitchers of water with slices of fruit in them are well received. You can find great combinations online—search for "infused water."

What does the pastor do during the dinner? This is not the time to isolate yourself in your office. Unless you have health issues, just take a few bites to tide you over—you can eat later. This is an opportunity to minister one more time to the grieving family, their relatives, and their friends. Grab a bottle of water or a cup of coffee and look for those who are alone (they are there!) and sit a few minutes with them. Then move on to the next table. You are not doing this to fish for compliments about the service but to care for them. Here is an acronym I picked up a long time ago from a soul-winning pastor: FORM. Ask them a question about their relationship to the Family, maybe a question about their work, their Occupation. One of our men likes to ask, "Do you consider yourself a spiritual person?" You are moving into the realm of Religion. Finally, what Message would you like to leave with them? A message of comfort will always be appropriate today, but they may ask you about your message a couple of hours ago. Be ready, be brief, and in just a few minutes, you can touch dozens of lives.

After the dinner is complete, you will discover that the immediate family is finalizing more details, gathering mementos they displayed, dividing up the flowers, and lingering a few more minutes with distant relatives. Do not rush them. Most of your workers have already left, but a couple of them should remain to help transport items to the cars and lock up the building.

I found these words by the author, Janet Beal, to be a fitting close to this chapter:

> Remember that the gift you are really giving to the family is lightening the load of heavy emotions and upsetting tasks at a time of sadness. This, as experienced caterers will tell you, is a time where the food runs last. People definitely need something to eat, but what they need more is the security and comfort that comes from knowing that someone has taken on the responsibility of all the details. Whether they notice your chicken divan is beside the point. What they will notice is the love, care and comfort you have provided in a difficult and painful time.[4]

Perhaps you will remember also that Jesus did not rebuke Martha for caring for the physical needs that He and the disciples had. He rebuked her for trying to take away Mary's time with the Savior. Providing a funeral dinner is a lot of work, but I hope you and your church will see it as a blessing to share and not as a burden to endure.

Funeral Meal Menus

Typically, the main entrée is purchased ready to eat, and the rest is donated.

The following menus work well in our part of the Midwest. If you need to adjust the menus to fit your families, what follows will at least give you a place to start in determining amounts.[5]

If you have larger groups, for example, seventy-five to one hundred or more, simply double or triple the amounts. The numbers given here will also leave some left over for workers and will allow for sending food home with the family.

- Low-budget: do not schedule the service near a meal time; provide fruit trays either from a store or given by the church family; cookies or pies; coffee, tea, water, and lemonade.
- Medium-budget: sandwich and relish trays can be added to the preceding.
- More money with less effort: consider having a restaurant cater the meal.[6]

Suggested Menus

Cold Cut Sandwiches for Twenty-Five

- 4–5 pounds of cold cuts (medium sliced)
- 2.5 pounds of cheese (medium sliced)
- 5 pints of salad (potato, macaroni, or coleslaw)
- 4 loaves of bread (sliced)
- 2 dozen dinner rolls (for small sandwiches)
- 4–5 dozen cookies or brownies
- 2 gallons of beverage

Ham Dinner for Forty

- 8 pounds of ham heated and sliced
- 1–2 packages of hamburger buns (some may want to make a sandwich) and condiments
- 2 dozen dinner rolls and butter
- 1 pasta and/or potato salad (assuming these and other dishes are large)
- 1 baked beans (two no. 10 cans will be more than enough)

- 1 green beans (eight 1-pound cans)
- 1 mashed potatoes (15–20 pounds) and/or a potato and cheese casserole
- 1 macaroni and cheese for children
- 1 relish tray
- 4 desserts: brownies, pudding, angel food cake, fruit salad

Fried Chicken Dinner for Fifty

- 100 chicken pieces (minimum)
- 20 pounds of mashed potatoes and a quart of gravy
- 1 chicken and noodles for children
- 2 large vegetable trays and dip
- 2 green leaf and 1 pasta salads
- 7 desserts
- 3 dozen bottles of water
- 5 two-liter bottles of soda pop (2 colas, 2 clear, 1 diet)

 CHAPTER TEN

THE FOLLOW-UP
After the Funeral, Now What?

It is Monday morning, and you are moving rather slowly around the house. You are exhausted physically, mentally, emotionally, and perhaps even spiritually; it seems like your tank is on empty. Yesterday, you preached twice and taught Sunday school as well. Last night, you had three families in your home for popcorn, pop, and fellowship, and no one was in a hurry to go home. It was great. Tuesday through Friday of last week were filled with study, administrative work, study, hospital visits, study, two committee meetings, a premarital counseling session, study, a marriage counseling session, and . . . study. Saturday you met with the men of the church for prayer, reviewed your Sunday school lesson, and tweaked your messages; moreover, sometime this past week, you managed to take your children to their music lessons and mow the lawn. No wonder you are worn out.

Now imagine this past week's flurry of activities, though very different in make-up, just as exhausting. It is Monday morning. The house has been cleaned by friends; the children somehow got up, got dressed, grabbed their lunches, and left for school. The refrigerator is filled with food that will last for a month or so it seems, but the house is quiet—very quiet—and it will be like this forever, for this past Saturday, you, along with two hundred family members and friends, buried your children's mother, your best friend, your sweetheart. Oh, it is so very quiet this morning. The company you work for has given you a couple more days at home. Your extended family has headed back to their homes and responsibilities. Your friends in town are back to their routine. You are here, sitting at the kitchen table as you have for the past fifteen years, but now for the first time, all alone.

Overwhelming loneliness is the reality of our parishioners a few days after they bury their loved ones, and like the rest of their family and friends, we have gotten back to our routine. The preparation for the funeral, the days of the visitation and funeral, are now over. It was exhausting. It was time consuming. You will be spending the next week or two catching up on other responsibilities put aside for those few days. Day off this week? It's not going to happen. You are back in your routine that has served you well, but one of your sheep is sitting at his kitchen table, where it is quiet, and he is all alone, the grief overwhelming. What can you do? What will you do?

Before we go any further into this chapter, I have a confession, Timothy. This chapter will be more about what has been discovered by research than personal testimony. If there is a part of the ministry to the grieving that I have often neglected, it is the days, the weeks, the months after. I am not alone in this, for half of those families who were surveyed indicated that their pastor never visited them after the funeral—not in the next week, the next month, or the year to follow.[1] To use James' words, "My brethren, these things ought not so to be."[2]

I am comfortable, maybe even skilled, in dealing with the preparations and the funeral, but afterward, with this Sunday's responsibilities and the next coming in a week, I get back into my routine, and I have often neglected the sheep. Thankfully, by the grace and plan of God, I am not the only one in their lives, but I am one who needs to be, and you must be, too. We need to determine how we as pastors and our churches can in a timely and effective manner minister to those who are hurting.

Our Foundation for the Follow-Up Days

You will recall that a dual theme has guided these chapters. We have the message of hope through the resurrection of our Savior, Jesus Christ, and the presence of God. These have been our foundational truths throughout our approach to walking with the saints in the shadows. Do not leave them in the pulpit or at the gravesite. Your presence over the next year will communicate the presence of God. Your attitude of hope will encourage the bereaved through their dark days. It will not be an easy transition for the grieving, but by the grace of God, and with a plan, you can, like a shepherd, lead them.

Most resources regarding funerals say very little about ministering to the family after the funeral; however, if we as pastors and our churches are the stewards of the Gospel, surely we ought to be involved in the lives of the grieving family and not just leave it to the professional grief counselors and agencies. Some excellent resources for attending to the family after the funeral are available in our community, and perhaps in yours, too—we identify them in "Resources" at the end of the book. If you lack the training and, at this point, your church cannot meet the family's need, these agencies can fill the gap; however, do not abdicate this important responsibility for ministering. This chapter will get you started, but do the hard work of preparing yourself and your church for future ministry.

A Godly Family Man's First Week Alone

Yesterday was Easter, or Resurrection Sunday, as our church likes to call it. Together we considered the disaster in the life of a man named Job. He was a rich man. He was a godly man. He was a family man. However, even though he was a rich, godly family man, or perhaps because he was all these things, in one day, he lost everything. It is devastation that none of us have ever experienced. How would you even dare to show up at this man's doorstep and try to offer him hope?

He was in the depths of grief, and his dear wife was no better off. Enter the three friends. This one act was the greatest and wisest thing these men could do for the man of God:

> Now when Job's three friends heard of all this evil that was come upon him, they came every one from his own place; Eliphaz the Temanite, and Bildad the Shuhite, and Zophar the Naamathite: for they had made an appointment together to come to mourn with him and to comfort him. And when they lifted up their eyes afar off, and knew him not, they lifted up their voice, and wept; and they rent every one his mantle, and sprinkled dust upon their heads toward heaven. So they sat down with him upon the ground seven days and seven nights, and none spake a word unto him: for they saw that *his* grief was very great. (Job 2:11-13)

As preachers, we often beat these friends up for the persecution they do to Job over most of the book. Their theologies were uninformed, to say the least, but as I have pointed out, we need to commend them for showing up, sitting down, and remaining silent for seven days. Those in our flocks who are hurting are comforted by the reality of the presence of God, and the presence of family, friends from church, and the pastor communicates this in no uncertain terms. Perhaps they will need to be reminded of the promises of the presence of God in the days ahead, but the most helpful thing we can do in the beginning is simply to be there.

We know Job had the hope of the resurrection, both his Redeemer's and his own, for he said,

> Oh that my words were now written! oh that they were printed in a book! That they were graven with an iron pen and lead in the rock for ever! For I know *that* my redeemer liveth, and *that* he shall stand at the latter *day* upon the earth: And *though* after my skin *worms* destroy this *body*, yet in my flesh shall I see God: Whom I shall see for myself, and mine eyes shall behold, and not another; *though* my reins be consumed within me. (Job 19:23-27)

He needed his friends, and they were there for him. They were there until the presence of God was revealed: "Then the Lord answered Job" (Job 38:1). By the end of the book, the LORD had ministered to Job in such a way that he could minister to his friends, and by the grace of God, his life was restored to his new normal.

The First Week

Maybe it will not be on a Monday, but within a few days, you will want to visit the house of mourning. Your time there will be appreciated. Make sure you do not give the impression that you are there to collect unpaid fees. You are there to communicate the presence of God and the love of church and pastor. It may be a time filled with remembering the loved one and naming people who had come from out of town. If the family members are not Christians, you may find an opportunity to share once again the Good News and the comfort that comes from knowing Christ.[3]

Visiting a non-Christian or nominal Christian family in the days following the funeral may be the time God will use you and your church to reach out and win them to Christ. They will have been wrestling with thoughts of their mortality and experiencing unrelenting loneliness. What better time to look for that opportunity to point them to the One Who will prepare them for eternity and Who promises never to leave them or forsake them.[4] Let me caution you, however, to be sensitive to the leading of the Holy Spirit. One of the best ways I have read for doing this is to follow the pattern laid out in Bill Hybels' book *Just Walk across the Room*. He admonishes the reader first to develop a friendship. You started to do this when you agreed to care for the loved one's funeral. Maybe you are already there, and now you can move to the next step: discover their story, that is, listen to them to learn where they are spiritually. Last, under the direction of the Spirit of God, discern the next step. Is it time to proclaim the Gospel, or do you take more time to develop the friendship or discover more of their story?[5]

The family who came from hundreds of miles away, the neighbor next door, the boss from work, and a friend from church have all helped in some way to minister to the grieving family. The visit from the pastor the day after or sometime during the following week will mean more, however, to this hurting individual or family than will ever be expressed.[6]

A few cautions are in order. Call them the night before to set up an appointment. Then, as in other visitation calls, if it is a widow or single woman, you will want to take your wife with you. I am probably an extremist, but I rarely embrace other women or children who do not share my last name and never without my wife, Debbie, being present. She is, of course, my designated hugger. The widow or the mother who has lost her child has arms that ache for her loved one, and your wife can fill that void for the time you are there. This is not a time to stay long, but in a half hour or so, you can share her grief and the Word as well as a time of prayer with her. If there are other nonpressing needs in the home, it would be appropriate to set up another appointment when the mourner is better able to focus on hearing counsel and making decisions. If you have not learned it before, you can easily discover during this first visit what kind of support the family has. This will enable you to plan types and frequencies of future visits.

The Following Weeks and Months

A common misconception is that a spouse, parent, or other family member will, like the rest of the mourners, "get over" the death and move on with his life; however, the future days hold markers that will remind him of his loved one's death, and the loneliness and grief will come to him again and again.[7] I remember the days and months following my mother's death. The month following was my birthday. It was at my birthday that I would always receive "our card" and a call from her—we had a card we both enjoyed and sent it back and forth for nearly fifteen years. Two months after my birthday was hers. Then came the holidays and other special occasions for my young family, when I would always call Mom and tell her all that was going on—only now she was gone, and once again, I ached. By the grace of God, Debbie would be there to comfort me, but what about your parishioners?

Liz Cowen Furman writes of two important actions we need to take for those who are grieving.[8] The second most important act is to be a listener. Often we do not know what to say. Perhaps we can follow the lead of Job's friends, who simply showed up, sat down, and said nothing. Furman then states the most obvious action we can take that we often minimize is to pray.[9] Do not underestimate the value of praying for your sheep and with your sheep. Everyone loves to hear her name, and how encouraging it is to hear her pastor carry her name to the throne of God that she might receive help in her time of need (Heb. 4:16). It is interesting that the word *need* in this verse is a verb that means "to use a rope or chain to frap a vessel," that is, to hold it together.[10] Since this family's life has just fallen apart, how appropriate that their shepherd would pray that God would give them the grace, the mercy, the help they need to hold it together.

In the early days and weeks to follow, you may witness expressions of grief that surprise or even shock you. Do not expect the family to react to this unnatural event in their lives as you or others would. The early Puritans were taught that any appearance of grief or sorrow was unacceptable.[11] If you walk into the home the first week and communicate that they need to "get it together," you will isolate them.[12] Take a quick walk through the psalms, and you will discover anger, vengeance, impatience, and much more. These godly men were not as limited in their emotional outbursts as we would expect. When death knocks at your parishioner's door, among other things, it creates an emotional crisis that must be worked through over time.[13] Your church and you as pastor need to be a community of care and compassion for the whole person—emotional, social, spiritual, and physical.[14] All of this will extend beyond that week of mourning and the Monday after.

> If a man beget an hundred *children*, and live many years, so that the days of his years be many, and his soul be not filled with good, and also *that* he have no burial; I say, *that* an untimely birth *is* better than he. For he cometh in with vanity, and departeth in darkness, and his name shall be covered with darkness. (Eccl. 6:3-4)

Though sometimes cynical in nature, the message of the preacher is that though a man has a hundred offspring, there will come a day when he will be remembered no more. That is not the case with the bereaved family to whom you have recently ministered. They remember everything, and every memory is enveloped with emotions. How can you as their pastor help them through this time? Mitchell and Anderson identify areas where they may need assistance. First, they need time and space to grieve, that is, *intervention*. Many have their expectations as to how they would want the grievers to act, and the family may need you to intervene to keep these "helpful" people from pressing the family. Second, the bereaved often need someone to acknowledge their grief and provide an opportunity to share those feelings. This is called *support*. The third need is to create memories that will comfort them in the days and years ahead. To *encourage* this will take some creativity, for example, a photo album, a tree planted in the loved one's honor, or a memorial gift to an institution. The last need is to begin *reintegration*. This may require your gentle confrontation.[15] As hard as it will be for the mourner, children are in the home, employment must be sought or returned to, and ministries once shared may need to be adjusted.

A dear friend from my youth married his high school sweetheart. They served the Lord together in their church for forty years, and then she died of cancer. He was asked what he would do now that she was gone. His answer was just what I expected from this godly man. He said, "We have spent our lives for the glory of God. Even in this illness, we made it our goal to glorify Christ. So that's what I will keep on doing—glorifying my Savior." Those words have often encouraged me in my "light afflictions."

Jay E. Adams, in his book *Shepherding God's Flock*, points out that often there is a fifth area of assistance that you as the bereaved's pastor can offer. Grief can lead to *change* that might not otherwise have been considered. He tells us this is more than just talking about change; we need to be there to help the family change. He lays out four steps. First, help the family set biblical objectives for the future; second, help them list problems or difficulties that will need to be overcome; third, discuss and decide upon the biblical solutions to those problems; and fourth, help them lay out a course of action to take, including the beginning steps, with dates to begin and when you will check back with them.[16] You might consider this way beyond your pay grade and that no one who is grieving is open to this, but I think we will both be surprised as to how God just might turn all these days of "ashes into beauty." Be prepared, Timothy, for this type of help as well as all the comforting that is needed.

Whether the death was sudden or expected for years, whether it was violent or the departed just did not wake up in the morning, the family will be hurting and in need of what could be called *healthy healing*. A checklist that your church family can follow in ministering to the bereaved would be beneficial.[17] You and your church family can communicate to them in myriad ways that they are not forgotten and neither is their beloved: a meal delivered and shared, cards sent to acknowledge significant events—birthdays, anniversaries, graduations—assisting with gardening and lawn care. The list is endless; the key is to communicate to this dear family that their church has not forgotten them.

Consider the following possibilities: periodic visits by the deacons and their wives in the home, an invitation to the widow or widower into your home for a meal, a letter of comfort, remembering birthdays and anniversaries, friends to sit with them at worship services, and of course including them on a weekly prayer list for a specified time, if your church publishes one. Your deacons and other trusted leaders can help you design a list of what your church family can successfully handle. How long will you keep this up—a month, a year, several years? It would be difficult to maintain this with multiple families indefinitely, but perhaps you can at least follow them for the first year. Some ministries offer classes on grieving, and you may want to consider this for your church. In our town, we have a funeral home owned and operated by Christians who offer multiple classes and events that minister to the families who have used their services as well as others. Perhaps you know one in your location or can work with a trusted director to create a ministry for your community. You would be wise to keep careful records of all the funerals in your congregation, whether you officiate them or not—record the departed's names and ages, the dates and locations of the funerals, messages preached, hymns sung, and so on. You will find this helpful as you work through your checklist.[18]

Guiding Principles for the Days Ahead

Delores Kuenning calls people like us "caregivers." She gives us a helpful list of do's and don'ts. She believes the most difficult of time for the mourners is seven to nine months after death. During those days, as well as before and after, you and your church family can communicate that you will be praying for them, you can share pleasant memories and words of admiration, share your tears, and listen without making judgments. Along with what you may do, do not avoid them because you do not know what to say. Do avoid meaningless if not unbiblical statements, for example, "time heals all wounds" or "I know how you feel." Do not change the subject when the griever wants to talk about the departed or attempt to counsel them with "get over it."[19]

Early in our marriage, Debbie and I experienced some of the most difficult events in our lives. Over the next forty years, there have been other times that our hearts have been broken and grieved. Some of them made sense as to why they took place, but others left us with more questions than answers. Why did our twin sons have to hang between life and death so early in life? Why did a godly husband and father have to be taken from our church when we all desperately needed him? There are more whys that have followed than I want to remember; however, what I have discovered is the truth that the Apostle Paul communicated to the church in Corinth: you and I need to go—we *must* go—through the "School for Comforters."[20]

> Blessed *be* God, even the Father of our Lord Jesus Christ, the Father of mercies, and the God of all comfort; Who comforteth us in all our tribulation, that we may be able to comfort them which are in any trouble, by the comfort wherewith we ourselves are comforted of God. For as the sufferings of Christ abound in us, so our consolation also aboundeth by Christ. And whether we be afflicted, *it is* for your consolation and salvation, which is effectual in the enduring of the same sufferings which we also suffer: or whether we be comforted, *it is* for your consolation and salvation. (2 Cor. 1:3-6)

As you spend time with the family, you will discover that the consolation, the comfort, you have received from the Lord and His saints will deepen your ability to help your congregation. You will be able to tell when some measure of healthy healing has taken place, and the church family can pare back their ministry to the family. There came a time when I understood that the memories and times of grief, though not as painful, would continue perhaps for the rest of my life, and so it will be in your parishioners' lives.

CHAPTER ELEVEN

YOUR FIRST FUNERAL

> The heart of the prudent getteth knowledge; and the ear of the wise seeketh knowledge.
>
> *Proverbs 18:15*

> Bow down thine ear, and hear the words of the wise, and apply thine heart unto my knowledge.
>
> *Proverbs 22:17*

Timothy, I have concluded that every funeral we oversee must offer hope to all who attend. As we have already considered, that hope is based on two unchanging facts: God is present, and Christ is alive! With this foundation, whatever your first funeral looks like or sounds like, your listeners will walk away with the opportunity to have comfort for that day and hope for eternity. In this chapter, we will walk through your first funeral, and along the way, you will hear the wisdom of fifty-five different pastors who have collectively officiated at thousands of funerals.[1] As I read their counsel to you in the surveys, I heard wisdom from above. Wisdom from God is characterized by meekness; it is gentle, without partiality and hypocrisy. These pastors did not come across as having arrived but as having come out from the presence of God.[2]

The First Steps

It is far more likely that you will have a funeral before you have a wedding. Perhaps at weddings you have attended, you noticed what took place throughout the event; however, at any funerals you have attended, it may have been you were one of the mourners and made no observations; you just experienced it. As always, when you lack wisdom, it is time to pray (James 1:5). More than one pastor who took this survey admonished us to start here. If there was ever a time you needed wisdom, Timothy, this is it.

Many of the pastors suggested that before you face your first funeral, you make certain preparations. For example, attend a funeral service before you must perform one. Sit in an inconspicuous place when a pastor friend is officiating. Assuming you do not know the family or the deceased, you can simply observe what takes place. Note any questions you may have and meet with that pastor the following week to have him walk you through what happened and why.

What part of the funeral makes you nervous? Prepare and then practice it before you need it. In the beginning, it is perfectly fine to use someone else's notes. In fact, in "Resources" at the end of the book, you will find several basic outlines for service orders and sermons that you can build on and make your own. You may find it helpful to use a book such as *The Star Book for Ministers* to get you started.[3] It is showing its age, but it has also passed the test of time. There are many other books designed to give you some direction. Peruse this book's bibliography and choose a couple to read early in your ministry. A funeral is not something you get a second chance with to minister to people who are grieving, so be prepared!

Before you read any further, have you taken the time to pray for God's comfort for the family and wisdom for you?

Though you have talked with him over the phone, if you have not met face-to-face with the funeral director of the home that will be caring for the deceased and his family, it would be good to stop by the day before the funeral to get better acquainted. Remember that you are both called to work with people in the community in their darkest hour—you are both there to serve. As you develop a relationship with him, it may go beyond your professional positions. Perhaps like one of the pastors from the survey discovered, the connection made with the director through the funerals may lead to his family attending church. Whether they come or not, it is simply good wisdom to get acquainted with your coworker.

Having exercised the ministry of presence at the hospital or the deceased's home, and having met with the family to discover their wishes, it is time for you to work on the service order. You may want to choose one from "Resources" or follow the pattern you observed officiated by your pastor friend. You will need to adapt to the age and cause of death of the deceased.[4] As in other public services, there is a starting point and an ending point. Like a sermon, there will be an introduction, a body, and a conclusion. Your first words can be a welcome and a thank-you on behalf of the family to those who came. The conclusion is often a time of prayer and assuring the family of your continued ministry in their lives. What about the body of the funeral? Unless the family has given you specific directions as to their desires, plan a service of no more than twenty minutes. Better for them to wish you had gone longer than for them to wish you had stopped long ago!

As you begin to fill in the body of the service with songs to be sung and Scripture to be read, remember you do not have to perform this whole service by yourself. Let the family be involved as much as they care to be. Perhaps individuals from your church who knew the deceased could also be a part of the service—to pray, to read Scripture, or to lead a congregational song. By involving others, you can spend the time you need on preparing a sermon that is not only personal but points the family and their friends to the God Who is there and the risen Christ, the only One Who can give hope both today and for the future.

Be sure to make multiple and abbreviated copies of the service order to distribute to the funeral director and other participants. It would also be good to share this ahead of time with the patriarch of the family to get his approval. This becomes your checklist to make sure those who were asked are actually going to participate and are ready. As you review the service order, take time to prepare any technology, such as microphones and recorded music, which needs to function flawlessly. If the technology is not ready or malfunctions, it will affect your confidence and that of the congregation.

One pastor's response is worth repeating word for word:

> Be prepared to give your entire day the day of the funeral. It may not take that long, but with your preparation, doing the service, and attending the dinner afterward, it may. You need to be there for the family. I find few things more exhausting than funerals, but I find few pastoral duties more fulfilling than being the spiritual support for a grieving family. People lean on their pastor at times of death harder than at any other time.[5]

You have arrived fifteen (I prefer thirty) minutes early at the funeral home, so the family and funeral director do not have to wonder whether you will be there.[6] You are wearing a dark suit, dress shirt ironed, shoes shined. You may find your area of the country is more relaxed in dress, but if in doubt, a suit is always, everywhere, acceptable. Determine that all participants are present and ready. Have you checked the pronunciation of names?[7] Listen! The music has been turned down by the funeral director, and this is your cue that the service is to begin. By the way, have you been praying?

The Funeral Service

As you approach the front of the room, it is a good time to pray. Perhaps stand a moment before the casket praying for those present and yourself. Now that you are behind the lectern, take a deep breath, look your audience in the eye, and, "Welcome and on behalf of the Wilson family, thank you for coming. We are here this morning not only to celebrate the life of Brother Dave but also to find comfort for today and hope for tomorrow."

Though you wrote out the service order and even what you will say word for word, do not be so rigid and formal that a smile or a laugh would seem out of place. The crowd that has gathered had a personal relationship with the departed and his family, and for a few minutes, they want you to come across as being personable, if not acquainted with their loved one. After the welcome, there can be a familiar hymn sung, a favorite and meaningful passage of Scripture read, a personalized review of the deceased's life, and a prayer of thanks for the life of the loved one. Remember to pray for the grace of God and wisdom for those who are left behind. This reminds me of a service where I greatly failed.

The deceased was in the middle of a difficult divorce, and they had minor children. The wife sat on one side of the room, the parents on the other. I was not sure how to relate to the wife, who wanted no contact with the parents or me, so not knowing what to do, I totally ignored her. That, my friend, was a mistake. If for no other reason than for her sake and that of the children, I could have said and prayed something like this: "Life is going to be very hard in the days ahead for [the mother's and father's names] children. [The mother's name] will need all the wisdom of God to meet their needs as their mother and due to the absence of their father. Let us pray for the children: [their names], [her name], and the grandparents who will all have a part in helping them through these difficult days."

You should know what is most significant to the families who had recently had a funeral.[8] This will help you to design and carry out the service. Sixty percent said the most meaningful part of the hours leading up to and including the funeral was the presence of their friends—not the words they spoke but just being there. Thirty-one percent said what they remembered most about the service was the music. As for the sermon, 18 percent stated that was what they remembered most. You can choose the songs prayerfully and carefully; however, make sure what they hear during the sermon is memorable and meaningful.

The message is the time to focus on their greatest needs—comfort for today and hope for tomorrow; therefore, exalt Christ and not the deceased. The living need to hear the hope of the Gospel. If you are unsure of the spiritual condition of the deceased, do not make a habit of "preaching them into heaven,"[9] neither should you "damn them to hell."[10] Your message is one of comfort in the Gospel, not primarily evangelism.[11] Use your Bible, but do not read a lot of verses—they will not remember them, and you do not have the time to expound on a large section of Scripture. Keep the message "short, simple and straightforward. People are not there to marvel at your preaching."[12] Because the last few days have been overwhelming, sleep has been fitful, and grief has distracted them, their ability to think clearly is diminished, and their minds will tend to wander. They will attach their minds onto seemingly insignificant points and illustrations. Do not shower them with hellfire and brimstone or soft-pedal the Gospel; rather, focus on the double foundation of the presence of God and the power of the risen Christ.

Timothy, I want to encourage you to write out the conclusion of your message word for word. It has happened all too often that we preachers have a hard time concluding. We are like the pilot who knows he must land the plane but cannot figure out how to get it down, so he just keeps circling the field. A simple review of your points and a personal illustration of application will get the job done, and your listeners will be able to remember that God is here and His Son is risen!

A final prayer is appropriate to acknowledge the presence of God and intercede on behalf of the family for wisdom and comfort. It also communicates to the director that the service is over and she can begin dismissing the guests. You will have shared this with her prior to the service and in your printed schedule.

One of the surveyed pastors summarized the funeral service this way: "Remember the threefold purpose of a memorial service in your planning: encourage the grieving, honor the life of the one who has passed, and warn and challenge the living to remember that they, too, will one day exit this world, Ecclesiastes 7:1-4."[13]

The Follow-Up

We have already addressed in an earlier chapter your actions after the service, so let me remind you of a few steps you will want to take. After your final prayer, walk over to the immediate family, warmly shake their hands, and assure them of your prayers and care for them. Then find a place to stand near the front and in the vicinity of the casket, but do not hover. Some will want to visit with you as they leave, but it is not the time to carry on a long conversation. You are there to communicate to the family that you are available, but you will also watch over the care of their loved one's remains.

After the guests and family members have been dismissed, the director, if not done before the service, will close the casket. She will then call for the pallbearers, and you will lead them to the hearse. Once the casket is secured, you will either be seated in the passenger side of the hearse or make your way to your car. If you are driving, the director will make sure you follow the lead car to the cemetery.

The graveside service should be very brief, unless there was not a service preceding. Typically, it consists of a Scripture reading, for example, 1 Corinthians 15:51–58, followed by pointing them to the resurrection and a prayer of commitment of the body to the care of God and for the comfort of the mourners. Spend a few moments with the principal mourners, and then step to the side. You may want to remain on site until the funeral party leaves.[14]

Make time for the family after the funeral. Go to the reception and visit them later (more than once) in their home, keeping them engaged in life. You do not have to have all the answers to their questions, but being there to weep with those who weep will be a testimony of the God Who is there in their lives. Not only will your presence give you the privilege of walking alongside them during this journey but it will gain you a greater understanding of their needs regarding their relationship with Christ and how to minister to them in the coming days.

Shortly after the funeral is also a good time for you to send a few thank-you cards. You will, of course, send a card to the family if they gave you an honorarium (you did not ask them for one, did you?).[15] A brief communication should be sent to those who participated in the service, church family members who assisted in various capacities (with music, in the kitchen, and in other areas, whether or not you asked them to assist), and even the funeral director. A brief personal note is good manners and will be very effective in paving the way for future contacts and opportunities to minister.

Timothy, though most of the time you will coordinate each part of the funeral with the director, there may be times you will need to work with law enforcement or military honor guards. There will be chaplains or commanders who will be able to help you work through plans. They are experienced and adept at serving grieving families as well as dealing with often complicated arrangements. Be open and humble enough to accept their advice and direction.[16]

If you prepared well and led a meaningful service, your act of ministry to the family will be remembered for years to come, and you will no doubt be called on the next time they have to walk through this valley filled with fears and shadows. These can be some of the most precious, though difficult, times you will spend with your flock. The more times you walk with them through this "unnatural" event, the greater they will love you for it.

> Yea, though I walk through the valley of the shadow of death, I will fear no evil: for thou *art* with me; thy rod and thy staff they comfort me. (Ps. 23:4)

> Two *are* better than one; because they have a good reward for their labour. For if they fall, the one will lift up his fellow: but woe to him *that is* alone when he falleth; for *he hath* not another to help him up. Again, if two lie together, then they have heat: but how can one be warm *alone*? And if one prevail against him, two shall withstand him; and a threefold cord is not quickly broken. (Ecc. 4:10–12)

> Then shall the King say unto them on his right hand, Come, ye blessed of my Father, inherit the kingdom prepared for you from the foundation of the world: For I was an hungred, and ye gave me meat: I was thirsty, and ye gave me drink: I was a stranger, and ye took me in: Naked, and ye clothed me: I was sick, and ye visited me: I was in prison, and ye came unto me.
>
> Then shall the righteous answer him, saying, Lord, when saw we thee an hungred, and fed *thee*? or thirsty, and gave *thee* drink? When saw we thee a stranger, and took *thee* in? or naked, and clothed *thee*? Or when saw we thee sick, or in prison, and came unto thee?

And the King shall answer and say unto them, Verily I say unto you, Inasmuch as ye have done *it* unto one of the least of these my brethren, ye have done *it* unto me. (Matt. 25:34-40)

EPILOGUE
Hope for Today and Tomorrow

> "There is the sense, the fear, that physical death is not natural, but an unnatural separation of that which belongs together." Falling in love, marriage, birth, and growing up—these are as natural as breathing in and out. But death? Death appears to be so out of order with the rest of God's creative acts.[1]

My dear Timothy, I want you to know that I have prayed for you and your ministry, especially since there will be significant times in the lives of your congregation both individually and collectively that you will especially need one another. Jesus said, "A new commandment I give unto you, that ye love one another; as I have loved you, that ye also love one another. By this shall all men know that ye are my disciples, if ye have love one to another" (John 13:34-35). God made us with the ability to love and to be loved, and He allows events into our lives that make it so valuable, even essential. Our Lord also made it clear that as your unsaved friends watch your congregation, the more they watch, the more likely they will be to arrive at the conclusion that there is a connection between you and Him.

These significant events are sometimes filled with joy: birthdays, anniversaries, graduations, and promotions. Sometimes they are filled with sorrow and unrelenting grief, and your church family will desperately need their brothers and sisters to come alongside to love them and to comfort them. Often we are at a loss as to how to provide that comfort to them. The good news is that most of the time, all you must do is just be there! It is called the *Ministry of Presence*.

> Chaplains who often must keep their theology to themselves have discovered that the Lord opens doors through the Ministry of Presence.[2]

Then there are other times we must speak. The Apostle Paul did this very thing by the direction of the Holy Spirit in 1 Thessalonians 4. The ancient world, like ours, could be very brutal with war, disease, family problems, and persecution. Add to that the false teachers, as in our day, who created many doubts about the loved ones who had died, and we understand why Paul wrote the following:

> But I would not have you to be ignorant, brethren, concerning them which are asleep, that ye sorrow not, even as others which have no hope. For if we believe that Jesus died and rose again, even so them also which sleep in Jesus will God bring with him. For this we say unto you by the word of the Lord, that we which are alive and remain unto the coming of the Lord shall not prevent them which are asleep. For the Lord himself shall descend from heaven with a shout, with the voice of the archangel, and with the trump of God: and the dead in Christ shall rise first: Then we which are alive and remain shall be caught up together with them in the clouds, to meet the Lord in the air: and so shall we ever be with the Lord. Wherefore comfort one another with these words. (1 Thess. 4:13-18)

> As we move into the age of the New Testament, it is this major event that cements the hopes of the Old Testament, emboldens the disciples of Christ, and brings believers comfort in the midst of their sorrows—the resurrection of our Savior, Jesus Christ.[3]

This is not a rebuke but a message of hope (1 Thess. 4:13-15). Paul is not intending to lay guilt on the church in Thessalonica for not knowing about this event. He wrote because it was part of the mystery of the end times that was just being revealed and also because they were babes in Christ. When your people are hurting is not the time to rebuke them; it is the time to comfort them.

> There is this deep contrast between the lost and the saved: for the lost, there is no hope, and for the believer, there is both comfort now and hope for the future. Dear Timothy, do not let your congregation leave the service, whether in the church, at the funeral home, or at the gravesite, without the hope of God's presence and the resurrection.[4]

The apostle wrote to the saints, "Let me tell you about those who are asleep in Jesus." Timothy, you and I know this. We read about it when Lazarus and Stephen died (John 11 and Acts 7). The body as when it is in repose is laid to rest in a cemetery, which literally means "a sleeping chamber." The soul and spirit that have separated from the body have gone to be with the Lord (2 Cor. 5:8).

The sorrow the saints experience can be overwhelming, but it can be tempered with the reality that their loved one still exists and is very much alive. Death for the believer is like sleep—the person still exists, and it is temporary. The Holy Spirit through Paul determined that you should clearly understand this truth. As a believer in Christ, you are not without hope. However, for the unbeliever, grief without hope assumes you will never see them again (Eph. 2:12). They are without Christ, without God, and without hope. For them, there is no assurance.

> In their book *All Our Losses, All Our Griefs*, Kenneth Mitchell and Herbert Anderson list a dozen emotions that people will experience in times of loss. When you arrive at the hospital or the home, you will see some or all of them played out before you. After the loved one dies, you can expect the emotions to come in a new wave: guilt, shame, loneliness, anxiety, anger, terror, bewilderment, emptiness, profound sadness, despair, and helplessness. "Grief is the clustering of some or all of these emotions in response to loss."[5]

Neither is Paul rebuking them for sorrowing. His words are to provide comfort. Christians grieve the loss of loved ones; it is normal, unavoidable. To have hope, that is, to have confident expectation in death, is to face it with submission and confidence in God. They are not gone; they only sleep.

God Gives Us Two Reasons to Hope

First is the certainty of the death, burial, and resurrection of Christ. On this foundation and your faith in this fact, you, too, will not only die and be buried but will also rise again.[6] "And if Christ be not raised, then they also which are fallen asleep in Christ are perished." But He is, and they are not! The second reason is the certainty of the rapture of the church. The sleep-death is not only sure; it is essential—that is, your body is not fit for eternity (1 Cor. 15:51-52). Those who are asleep in Jesus, God will bring with Him, and in the twinkling of an eye, the spirit will be united with the body and transformed into a body that will last forever. Moreover, we who are alive and are waiting for that event to take place will also be transformed into an eternal body, and so shall we ever be with the Lord.

> There is coming a time, because of the death, burial, and resurrection of Christ, that there will no longer be a need for all of these services. As it says in Revelation 21:4, "And God shall wipe away all tears from their eyes; and there shall be no more death, neither sorrow, nor crying, neither shall there be any more pain: for the former things are passed away." But for now, you are needed to walk with the sheep through this dark valley, to help them face their enemy, Death, and to introduce them to the One Who can give them hope.[7]

Two reasons to hope: the death, burial, and resurrection of Christ and the rapture of the church. Actually, there is a third reason to hope—you have God's Word on it (1 Thess. 4:15). The apostle is answering a question or an issue that was important to the Thessalonian church. Many had died, and there was an air of hopelessness. This "Word of the Lord" until then had been a mystery, but no longer. Through Paul, God gave this new revelation: for those of you who are alive when the Lord returns, your loved ones will not be left behind. As a matter of fact, you will not be raptured without them. You will not be snatched first; you have to wait in line, and then together you will be with the Lord forever. You have God's Word on it!

> I have been disappointed many times at the funerals I have attended that this crowning truth, this fundamental of the faith, is never even mentioned—not even in passing! My dear Timothy, if there is no resurrection, if Christ is not raised from the dead, then you have no message of hope.[8]

God Walks You through This Message of Hope (1 Thess. 4:16–18)

How will this message of hope be fulfilled? First, you will hear an announcement: "For the Lord himself shall descend from heaven with a shout, with the voice of the archangel, and with the trump of God: and the dead in Christ shall rise first" (1 Thess. 4:16). Notice, it is the Lord Himself! He will not send His angels. The Bridegroom is coming for His Bride!

> You will be tempted to dance around death by spending much time on memorializing the one departed. You will offer words of solace by speaking of that beloved father or grandfather being in the presence of God in a place called Heaven. Memorializing the departed and comforting the sorrowing can and must be done. But remember, without the resurrected Christ, the One Who has defeated the final enemy, there is no foundation for hope. Make much of the One Who died and rose again, and you will offer hope in sorrow and the presence of the living Christ in the pain of the moment.[9]

His coming is simultaneous with a very dramatic announcement like the command of a general to his army. Hear the authority of Jesus' command recorded in John 11:43: "Lazarus, come forth!" The sound of that voice will summon all the dead in Christ to rise out of their graves.

> After this I looked, and, behold, a door was opened in heaven: and the first voice which I heard was as it were of a trumpet talking with me; which said, Come up hither, and I will shew thee things which must be hereafter. (Rev. 4:1)

He who spoke the world into existence can handle this "small task."

> Behold, I shew you a mystery; We shall not all sleep, but we shall all be changed, In a moment, in the twinkling of an eye, at the last trump: for the trumpet shall sound, and the dead shall be raised incorruptible, and we shall be changed. (1 Cor. 15:51–52)

Notice Paul said "we." He fully expected Christ to return in his lifetime. When that takes place—here is the best part—we will experience the eternal presence of Christ (1 Thess. 4:17). Paul calls this for the believer the "blessed hope." What is it that makes this such a wonderful event in the life of the believer? Is it that we are "out of here"? Is it that it begins the time with no more pain, no more tears, and no more suffering? Is it our anticipated new home? All of these are true, but the real reason is that we are going to see Jesus Christ, and we will be with Him for all of eternity. Heaven is not heaven because of the streets of gold. It is not about the mansion that has been built and is waiting for us. It is all about Him! What can you do with a message like this? Comfort one another. "Wherefore comfort one another with these words" (1 Thess. 4:18).

It is comforting to know that the Bridegroom provides comfort for his Bride. Let me remind you of the purpose of this passage. It is not for winning a theological argument regarding eschatology. It is for comfort. O Timothy, comfort those who have lost loved ones. Comfort those who are being persecuted. Comfort those who are weary of this world. Comfort those who wait for their loved one's imminent death.

My dear friend, when you see your brother or sister hurting, comfort him or her with these words. It is not the time for a rebuke but for you to come alongside and remind your brother or sister that Jesus is alive and that He is very near.

> We have the message of hope through the resurrection of our Savior, Jesus Christ, our own resurrection, and the presence of God. These have been our foundational truths throughout our approach to walking with the saints in the shadows. Do not leave them in the pulpit or at the gravesite. Your presence over the next year will communicate the presence of God. Your attitude of hope will encourage the bereaved through their dark days. It will not be an easy transition for the grieving, but by the grace of God, and with a plan, you can, like a shepherd, lead them.[10]

My Final Admonishment to You

My dear Timothy, compared to you, my race is almost over. If the Lord Jesus should tarry a little longer, you will have so many opportunities to minister to the grieving, to give them hope for today and for tomorrow. It has been my prayer and purpose to provide for you the guidance I received from so many godly men and of course the Lord Himself. Now what will you do with it? I want to offer you one last word, the same guidance Moses' father-in-law, Jethro, gave to him. "If thou shalt do this thing, and God command thee *so*, then thou shalt be able to endure, and all this people shall also go to their place in peace" (Exod. 18:23).

When faced with your very first funeral, review the instructions given in this text and ask the Lord if you should follow one or more of the points you have learned. If He gives you confirmation through His Word and by His Spirit that you should, then God has answered my prayer. If He leads you in another direction, even then, let us praise His Name together that God's children have received hope for today and the unsaved man, woman, or child has received hope for tomorrow.

> If you prepared well and led a meaningful service, your act of ministry to the family will be remembered for years to come, and you will no doubt be called on the next time they have to walk through this valley filled with fears and shadows. These can be some of the most precious, though difficult, times you will spend with your flock. The more times you walk with them through this "unnatural" event, the greater they will love you for it.[11]

RESOURCES

Service Orders

Service

Service 1

    Organ Music
    Introductory Statement (an appropriate verse of Scripture)
    Scripture and Prayer
    Vocal Music (solo, duet, trio)
    Message
    Vocal Music
    Prayer and Benediction[1]

Service 2

    Prayer
    Obituary
    Hymn: "In the Garden"
    Personal Testimony Written by the Deceased
    Poem
    Hymn: "O Come All Ye Faithful"
    Message
    Solo
    Family Tradition (reading of Christmas story and prayer)
    Testimonies
    Solo
    Prayer[2]

Service 3

    Choir
    Welcome
    Hymn
    Prayer
    Choir
    Scripture Reading
    Family Eulogies
    Hymn
    Duet
    Message
    Prayer[3]

Service 4

    Scripture Reading
    Musical Selection (if requested)
    Prayer
    Obituary
    Prayer
    Message
    Musical Selection (if requested)
    Benediction[4]

Service 5

    Call to Worship
    Obituary
    Psalm 28:1, 2, 6–9
    Invocation
    Hymn: "In the Garden"
    Shortened List of Scriptures
    Scripture Reading: Psalm 27
    Solo: "Amazing Grace"
    Sharing (children and grandchildren)
    Scripture Reading: John 14:1–6, 15–27
    Solo: Psalm 23
    Meditation
    Organ Solo: "My Father Planned It All"

Committal (done here due to private burial)
Benediction

Service 6

Hymn: "It Is Well with My Soul" (one stanza)
Welcome
Scripture Reading: Psalm 23
Eulogy
Special: "Jesus Loves Me"
Reading: "Footprints in the Sand"
Special: "It Is Well with My Soul"
Message
Memories (invite a few family members or friends to share a memory)
Closing Instrumental Hymn: "At Calvary"

Service 7

Opening and Welcome
Scripture Reading
Sharing of Memories
Scripture Reading
Message
Closing Hymn

Service 8

Welcome
Prayer
Scripture
Memories/Tributes
Message
Closing

Service 9

Organ Prelude
Scripture
Prayer
Obituary

Song or Special Music
Message
Benediction

Service 10 (Unsaved)

Psalm 23
Prayer
Hymn: "Amazing Grace"
Scripture Reading: Romans 8:21–28
Hymn: "The Old Rugged Cross"
Eulogy
Scripture Reading: 1 Peter 1:3–9
Scripture Lesson: "Heaven Is a Destination" (John 14)
Hymn: "In the Garden"
Committal
Closing Prayer

Graveside

Graveside 1

Hymn
Scripture
Brief Comment
Committal
Prayer

Graveside 2

Scripture
Remarks (brief)
Military Honors
Prayer
Benediction

Graveside 3

Military Honors
Scripture

Brief Comments on Scripture
Prayer

Hymns for Funeral Services

Abide with Me
All the Way My Savior Leads Me
Christ Arose
Christ the Lord Is Risen Today
Close to Thee
Face to Face
Fairest Lord Jesus
God Will Take Care of You
Great Is Thy Faithfulness
Guide Me, O Thou Great Jehovah
He Hideth My Soul
He Leadeth Me
He the Pearly Gates Will Open
How Great Thou Art
I Know That My Redeemer Lives
I Know Whom I Have Believed
I Need Thee Every Hour
It Is Well with My Soul
It May Be at Morn
I Will Sing the Wondrous Story
Now I Belong to Jesus
One Day
Only Trust Him
O That Will Be Glory for Me
Rock of Ages
Savior, Like a Shepherd Lead Us
Shall We Gather at the River
Since I Have Been Redeemed
Surely Goodness and Mercy
Sweet By and By
The Solid Rock
The Strife Is Over
To God Be the Glory
Trusting Jesus
Turn Your Eyes upon Jesus

What a Wonderful Savior
What If It Were Today?
When the Roll Is Called
When We All Get to Heaven[5]

Scriptures to Use for Readings, Messages, and Counseling

Deuteronomy 30:15-20	The Decisions We Make
2 Samuel 12:16-23	The Death of a Child
Job 19:23-27	I Know My Redeemer Lives!
Psalm 8	We Are on His Mind
Psalm 23	The Lord Is My Shepherd
Psalm 25	Look upon Me in My Affliction
Psalm 34:1-19	The Goodness of Our God
Psalm 37	Trusting in the Lord
Psalm 46	God Is Our Refuge
Psalm 61	You Are My Shelter and Strong Tower
Psalm 62	The Lord Only Is My Rock and Salvation
Psalm 90	Numbering Our Days
Psalm 91	The Security of God's Children
Psalm 100	Knowing the Lord
Psalm 103	The Benefits of Knowing the Lord
Psalm 116	Precious in the Sight of the Lord
Psalm 139	O Lord, You Know Me
Psalm 145	From Generation to Generation
Ecclesiastes 3:1-3	To Everything There Is a Season
Ecclesiastes 7:1-4	The Day of Death Is Better than a Birthday
Isaiah 40:1-11, 28-31	The Message of God's Comfort
Isaiah 43:1-5	You Shall Not Be Burned
Nahum 1:7	Discovering Again That the Lord Is Good
Matthew 6:9-13	The Lord's Prayer
John 3:16, 36	The Love of God
John 5:24-29	(committal service)
John 10	The Good Shepherd
John 11:11-26	The Promise of the Resurrection
John 11:35-36	Jesus Wept

John 14:1–31	Jesus' Words of Comfort[6]
John 20:1–18	The Resurrection of Jesus
Romans 8:14–39	The Power of God over Death
Romans 8:18–28	The Wonders of God's Providence
Romans 8:35–39	The Love of God
1 Corinthians 15:20–58	The Certainty and Manner of the Resurrection
1 Corinthians 15:51–58	The Power of God over the Grave[7]
2 Corinthians 5:1–10	A Building from God—in the Heavens
Ephesians 2	The Wonders of His Grace
Philippians 1:12–23	A Believer's Death
1 Thessalonians 4:13–18	Wherefore Comfort One Another
2 Timothy 4:6–8	A Faithful Finish
1 John 3:1–3	The Joy of Belonging to Him
Revelation 4:13	Blessed Are the Dead
Revelation 21–22	The Amazing Future[8]

Sermon Starters and Abbreviated Outlines

You might find sermon starters and outlines from your own daily Bible readings, sermons, and devotional books. Examples from my own include the following:[9]

No More Tears

> And God shall wipe away all tears from their eyes; and there shall be no more death, neither sorrow, nor crying, neither shall there be any more pain: for the former things are passed away. (Rev. 21:4)

Surely this is one of the most glorious promises in the Bible! No more suffering, no more sorrow, no more death! In this present life, in this present world, every one of us must endure suffering and sorrow to various degrees and, eventually, death. But our gracious Savior "hath borne our griefs, and carried our sorrows," and because "the LORD hath laid on him the iniquity of us all . . . he was cut off out of the land of the living" (Isa. 53:4, 6, 8), and He endured for us the awful suffering of death on the cross.[10]

The King of Terrors
John 11:1–46

Introduction

1. It is at this moment of time that the words of Scripture become very meaningful and comforting to the believer.
2. I have often prayed for others that God would give them grace for living and grace for dying, but how do you pray for those who helplessly stand by and watch?
3. READ John 11:1-17.
4. If the Son of God is not victorious over the King of Terrors, then He is not the Lord of lords, nor the King of kings, nor the Son of God!

I. THE SON OF GOD AND DEATH AND DYING, vv. 1-17

   a. There are some things we understand about death and dying.
   b. We know these things, but we struggle when death knocks at our door!
   c. Was Jesus callous toward His friends? Was He powerless? No!

II. THE SON OF GOD AND DEATH AND DOUBT, vv. 18-38

   a. During the days following Lazarus' death, you will see grief and tears, confidence and doubts.
   b. The first one we meet after the funeral is a sister, Martha, vv. 17-22.
   c. Next, we meet Martha's sister Mary, vv. 31-32. READ
   d. Then there are those that day who were filled with doubts, v. 37. READ
   e. How will you face the death of your beloved friend? How will you face your own? Unshakeable faith? Disappointment? Or soul-shattering unbelief?

III. THE SON OF GOD AND DEATH DEFEATED, vv. 39-46

   a. If not for what I'm about to read, life and death would be frightening—terrifying!

      b. Jesus has made it very clear, the gates of hell cannot prevail against Him; death cannot hold Him or deter Him. He is the Resurrection and the Life!
      c. If He is not the Son of God Who can and does defeat death, then everything said about Him is a lie.

Conclusion

1. My friends, this event was recorded for you that you might believe that Jesus is the Christ, the Son of God, and that by believing you would have life through His name.
2. And for those of us who know Christ as Savior, it is a wonderful comfort to know that Jesus loves us and not only lovingly cares for our loved ones who have died but will give us the strength and grace we need to go on living.

A Kindred Spirit with Philip
Acts 8

Introduction

1. When I thought about our dear sister and spoke with her family, her love of horses came to mind. It reminded me of a man in the Bible whose name means just that—"a lover of horses."
2. He is found in Acts chapter 8, and his name is Philip. And as I thought about this man and Donna, I discovered there were several similarities.

I. THEY BOTH WERE BUSY HELPING OTHER PEOPLE

      a. Philip was serving the Lord in a city called Samaria.
      b. He was preaching and teaching and helping as many people as he could. It says that because of his ministry in Samaria, "there was great joy in that city."
      c. In the elementary school where this young mother served as a teacher's aide, "there was great joy in that school."

II. THEY BOTH WERE SENT TO HELP ONE PERSON

    a. In verse 26 of Acts 8, we read that God sent Philip from the busy city of Samaria where he knew many people to minister to someone he did not know.
    b. The man God sent him to help was one who was searching for answers, searching for God, and God sent him a man.
    c. Even in her weakened condition, Donna took walks at the mall. During her walks, she handed individual people a little booklet, a Gospel tract.
    d. Just touching one life at a time by taking the time to put in their hands a message that would help them and change their lives for eternity.

III. THEY BOTH HAD THE SAME MESSAGE

    a. The message in the Gospel tract is the same message that Philip preached in busy Samaria and on a lonely highway in southern Israel.
    b. READ Acts 8:29–35
    c. Beginning where Philip found this official of Egypt reading in the book of Isaiah, he preached unto him Jesus.
    d. Jesus—the Son of God, the Lamb of God and the risen Savior, is victorious over death, hell, and the grave, and now He is in heaven.
    e. That chance meeting between Philip and the Ethiopian changed the man's life forever. For Jesus said, "He that believes in me, has everlasting life."

IV. THEY BOTH HAVE LEFT TO SERVE IN ANOTHER PLACE

    a. The last thing that Philip and Donna have in common is that they both have left to serve in another place.
    b. When Philip left the Ethiopian, he began to serve the Lord in another place over fifty miles away, and we do not read about him again for over thirty years.
    c. When Donna passed away a few days ago, she left to serve the Lord in another place, and perhaps for some of us, it will be thirty years before we see her again.
    d. But I want you to note the impact that Philip left on the

Ethiopian: "he went on his way rejoicing," and your life has been enriched because of your chance meeting with Donna.

Conclusion

1. The question is, will you leave today to "go on your way rejoicing"?
2. Rejoicing in the memories and kindnesses that this lady showed you? Rejoicing in knowing that Donna is in a better place where there is no more pain, no more suffering?
3. Or will you rejoice because the message that Donna carried in her heart and her hand, the message of Who Jesus is and what He has done for you, has found its way in your heart?
4. Can you say like the Ethiopian, like Donna, "I believe that Jesus Christ is the Son of God"?

Safely Home
Psalm 23

Introduction

1. It was true of my parents; it's true of Debbie and me. When our sons and their families take a long trip, we always want to hear when they have safely arrived at their vacation spot and especially when they arrive safely home.
2. Precious words to hear: "safely home." On Monday, we received word regarding Melanie that she was safely Home.
3. In Psalm 23:6, we read . . .
4. In this Psalm, you are promised the eternal presence of the eternal God from this moment until you are safely home, for . . .

I. GOD WANTS YOU WITH HIM

   a. Notice the personal pronouns throughout this Psalm.
   b. He wants to have a personal relationship with you.
   c. Have you ever invited God to be a part of your life?
   d. God has invited *you* to be a part of *His* life!
   e. And for all eternity, He wants you to be with Him!

II. GOD WANTS YOU TO DWELL WITH HIM

    a. Jesus speaks of abiding with Him.
    b. *To abide* means "to be at home with."
    c. Are you "at home with" the idea of God being a part of your day, every day, all day? Does the thought of being Home with God for eternity thrill you or frighten you?
    d. David said, "I will dwell in the house of the Lord."

III. GOD WANTS YOU TO DWELL IN HIS HOUSE

    a. This word, *house*, means exactly that: a house.
    b. It does not mean just stopping by for a visit or spending the night.
    c. It means being a member of His family—enjoying His protection, the provisions made for family members, and the fellowship of all who dwell there.
    d. It means to be at home with God—forever!

Conclusion

1. Only one with a personal relationship with God could view the death of a loved one as being precious, because that person is safely Home.
2. Can you say with that same assurance "the Lord is my shepherd" and one day, even as you pass through death's door, know you will be safely Home?
3. Jesus was the One Who paid for your safe passage to Home. He was the One Who died for your sins and was buried and rose again that when your time comes to leave this world, you might go safely Home.
4. If I can help you with that decision, let me know before you leave today, so that no matter where your travels take you, you will be finally, safely, Home. I invite you to receive Jesus Christ as your personal Savior.

What the Lord Jesus Wants You to Know

Right now, it might be very difficult even to think. You might not feel like you have the emotional energy to concentrate on things. Thinking about

things is difficult. However, if you could quiet your heart and think about three wonderful things for just a few moments, it will help you right now and in the days ahead. Think of these three things:[11]
1. The Lord Jesus truly **cares** for you (Ps. 55:22; 1 Pet. 5:7).
2. The Lord Jesus truly desires to **comfort** you (Matt. 9:22; Ps. 119:76).
3. If you know Christ as your Savior, the Lord Jesus truly will **come** for you (John 14:1-3).

Going Home
John 14:1–3

What do you think of when you hear the word *home*? For some, home was not a happy place. For others, there were times of laughter and sharing. Regardless of what home was like for you, if you know Christ as your Savior, heaven is a special place. It is your home.[12]
1. The **peace** that the Lord Jesus wants to give to us right now (John 14:1, 27).
2. The **place** that the Lord Jesus describes for us (John 14:2).
3. The **preparation** that the Lord Jesus is undertaking for us (John 14:3a).
4. The **promise** that the Lord Jesus gives to us (John 14:3b).
5. The very best part of our Heavenly Home is the **presence** of the Lord Jesus with us (John 14:3c).

It's Growing Strong in My Heart!

There are changes taking place in our lives every day. Right now, you are in a very major change, a difficult change. For the next few moments, please allow me the privilege to share with you what's growing in my heart, in spite of difficult changes.[13]
1. The older I grow, I am finding myself growing in **amazement** (1 Tim. 1:14-16).
2. The older I grow, I am finding myself growing in **assurance** (2 Cor. 4:16-18).
3. The older I grow, I am finding myself growing in **appreciation** (John 14:1-3).
4. The older I grow, I am finding myself growing in **anticipation** (2 Cor. 5:1-9).

End-of-Life and Bereavement Resources

American Association of Retired Persons (AARP) Widowed Persons Service, 601 E Street, NW, Washington, DC 20049. (800) 687-2277. http://www.aarp.org/griefandloss/organization.html[14]

Blake, Keith. *Widow's Might for the 21st Century*. 2009. A ministry devoted to helping people discover ways to better meet the needs of those who are widowed. http://www.widowsmight21st.com/.

Hospice of Central Ohio, 2069 Cherry Valley Road, Newark, OH 43055. (740) 788-1400. http://www.hospiceofcentralohio.org/. "We believe that everyone should have access to end-of-life care regardless of their ability to pay, complexity of care, or severity of need. Working together, we can ensure that all eligible patients have a meaningful end-of-life experience and the opportunity to write the last chapter of their life." HOCO is one of the local hospice organizations in our city. There are hospice organizations throughout the United States under different names. https://www.hospicefoundation.org/. You can also check with your hospital's social work office to get in contact with them. It is my experience that they provide a wonderful service to the critically ill and their families with inpatient and home care.

Journey in Grief Care, 13202 Word of Life Drive, Hudson, FL 34669. (727) 856-3530. http://www.griefcarefellowship.org/. Grief Care Fellowship has produced thirty-six DVD training sessions, student notebooks, and textbooks authored by Dr. H. Norman Wright, grief and trauma therapist. "Curriculum for training your church to minister to those who have lost loved ones—with knowledge, skill, and compassion."[15]

Newsletters, Websites, and Blogs to Help You Help Those Who Grieve

Though you will find these resources interesting and helpful, their listing here is not to be construed as a blanket recommendation.

Frontline newsletter is available through professional caregivers. Check with your local funeral home or contact office@verheyden.org.

My Careletter, Guiding Me through Life's Passages. Check with your local funeral homes.

Wilde, Caleb. "Confessions of a Funeral Director." Facebook.

Haugk, Kenneth C., founder. Stephen Ministries. http://www.stephenministries.org/. This Christian training organization located in St. Louis, Missouri, provides resources for churches, for example, *Journeying through Grief.*

Dougy Center, National Center for Grieving Children and Families. http://www.dougy.org/. Provides help for children grieving.

Challies, Tim. http://www.challies.com/. Canadian pastor who writes this daily blog.

Jackson, Susan. The Grieving Path: A Journey through Grief to Healing. http://grievingpath.com/index.php/daily-bread. Dedicated to parents who have lost a child.

Funeral and Memorial Information Council. https://www.talkofalifetime.org/. FAMIC is a membership organization comprising organizations in nearly all areas of the death care industry.

InSight. https://www.insightbooks.com/celebrants. An InSight Certified Celebrant is a person who has been trained and certified through InSight to meet the needs of families during their time of loss. A Funeral Celebrant serves by providing a funeral service, memorial service, or tribute that is personalized and individualized to reflect the personality and lifestyle of the deceased after consultation with the family and loved ones and coordination with the funeral home.

CaringInfo. https://www.nhpco.org/patients-and-caregivers/. CaringInfo provides information and support for anyone who is planning ahead, caregiving, living with a serious illness, or grieving a loss.

NOTES

Introduction
1. This conclusion is the result of the reading I have done, the chaplain training I have received, the testimonies I have heard, and the emphasis of Scripture.
2. John 11:1-7, 11-17 (KJV).
3. Job 18:14. Barnes, *Barnes' Notes*; Henry, *Matthew Henry's Commentary on the Whole Bible*; Jamison et al., "Job," in *Commentary Critical and Explanatory on the Whole Bible*, https://www.biblestudytools.com/commentaries/jamieson-fausset-brown/job.
4. "The symbol of 'sleep' for *death* is common to all languages, and familiar to us in the Old Testament." Jamison et al., "Matthew," in *Commentary Critical and Explanatory on the Whole Bible*, https://www.biblestudytools.com/commentaries/jamieson-fausset-brown/matthew. "Because of the resemblance between them, as sleep is the 'kinsman of death.' In this sense it is often used by pagan writers. However, in the Scriptures it is used to intimate that death will not be final: that there will be an awaking out of this sleep." Barnes, *Albert Barnes' Notes*. This provides the foundation of my second conclusion that must be emphasized at the funeral.
5. John 11:39.
6. John 11:18-22.
7. John 11:23-27.
8. John 11:31-32.
9. "The gates of hell" are not, as commonly believed, a reference to Satan and his power but a metaphor for death, i.e., through death, "the gate," entrance is made into hell. Clarke, *Adam Clarke's Commentary on the Bible*. "Some explain it (gates of hell) of 'the assaults of the powers of darkness'; but though that expresses a glorious truth, probably the former (gates of death) is the sense here." Jamison et al., "John," in *Commentary Critical and Explanatory on the Whole Bible*, https://www.biblestudytools.com/commentaries/jamieson-fausset-brown/john.

10. John 11:38-44.
11. 1 Cor. 15:55-57.
12. https://www.goodreads.com/author/quotes/159003.Richard_Baxter.

Chapter 1

1. Berkoff, *Systematic Theology*, 261.
2. Gen. 2:7ff.
3. Gen. 2:7, "form," yâtsar, through the *squeezing* into shape; to *mould* into a form; especially as a *potter*. Strong, *Strong's Expanded Exhaustive Concordance of the Bible*, s.v. "formed."
4. Ps. 139:14.
5. Gen. 3:22-23.
6. Gen. 3:17-19.
7. Bancroft, *Elemental Theology*; Chafer, *Systematic Theology*, 7:114; Thiessen, *Introductory Lectures in Systematic Theology*, 367-69.
8. Gen. 5:5.
9. Geisler, *Systematic Theology*, 3:123.
10. Gen. 3:15; Gal. 4:4; Matt. 1:18; Bancroft, *Elemental Theology*, 123-30.
11. John 3:14-15; Heb. 2:14, 10:5-9; Bancroft, *Elemental Theology*, 164-89; Thiessen, *Introductory Lecture*, 312-15.
12. "Healthcare Costs," Centers for Medicare and Medicaid Services, https://www.cms.gov/research-statstics-data-and-systems.
13. "Funeral Costs," Smart Asset, https://smartasset.com/life-insurance. For more statistics, see the National Funeral Directors Association, http://www.nfda.org/.
14. 1 Cor. 15:26.
15. Strong, *Strong's Expanded Exhaustive Concordance of the Bible*, s.v. "the last enemy."
16. Ryrie, *A Survey of Bible Doctrine*, 62-64. See Cairns, *Christianity through the Centuries*, 481.
17. Gen. 4:8-10.
18. Strong, *Strong's Expanded Exhaustive Concordance of the Bible*, s.v. "mourn," "weep."
19. Strong, s.v. "Heth."
20. Murphy, *Barnes' Notes*, 346-47.
21. Gen. 49:29.
22. Gen. 50.
23. McClendon, *Doctrine*, 2:83.
24. Strong, *Systematic Theology*, 2:656.
25. Luke 16:19-31 is not a parable but the account of actual men and what became of them at death. Wiersbe, *Be Courageous*, 41-47; Thiessen,

Introductory Lectures, 451, 488–89.
26. John 16:12–13.
27. Mark 12:18.
28. Acts 23.
29. Cairns, *Christianity through the Centuries*, 117.
30. Rom. 5:12.
31. McClendon, *Systematic Theology*, 2:84.
32. 1 John 2:2.
33. 1 Cor. 15:5–8.
34. 1 Thess. 4:13.

Chapter 2

1. Akin Oyedele, "It's Gotten a Whole Lot More Expensive to Die in America," October 31, 2017, http://www.businessinsider.com/. Caskets and services have risen 230 percent from 1986 to 2016.
2. "Where Do Americans Die," Stanford School of Medicine, https://palliative.stanford.edu/home-hospice-home-care-of-the-dying-patient/where-do-americans-die.
3. Rom. 12:15.
4. Schaeffer, *Affliction*, 21.
5. Schaeffer, 26.
6. Mitchell and Anderson, *All Our Losses*, 35–46.
7. Winokuer and Harris, *Principles and Practices of Grief Counseling*, 98.
8. Winokuer and Harris, 99–100.
9. *Merriam-Webster's Collegiate Dictionary*, s.v. "cope."
10. Bunyan, *Pilgrim's Progress*, 16–17.
11. Woodard, *Ministry of Presence*.
12. Heb. 13:5; John 10:4, 27–30; Rom. 8:35–39.
13. John 11:25.
14. Rom. 8:22–23.
15. 2 Cor. 2:12–16; 4:3–5.
16. Mitchell and Anderson, *All Our Losses*, 139.
17. Mitchell and Anderson, 143.
18. Furman, *How to Plan a Funeral*, 26–30.
19. Furman, 61–66.
20. Rom. 5:2; 1 Cor. 13:13; 2 Cor. 10:15; Gal. 5:5; Col. 1:23; 1 Thess. 1:3; 5:8; 1 Pet. 1:21.
21. Mitchell and Anderson, *All Our Losses*, 145.
22. Jude 1:20–23.
23. 1 Cor. 12.
24. Adams, *Christian Counselor's Manual*, 414.

25. Fitzgerald, *Mourning Handbook*, 73.
26. Sanders, *Grief*. For more reading on helping those who grieve, see Worden, *Grief Counseling and Grief Therapy*; Kubler-Ross, *On Death and Dying*; Bridges, *Trusting God*; Saxman, "Ministering to Those Who Mourn," 12–14; Gorman, "When a Child Dies."
27. For resources on helping those who grieve, see Wolfelt, "Helping Homicide Survivors Heal"; Wolfelt, *Understanding Your Grief*; Wolfelt, *Handbook for Companioning the Mourner*; Wolfelt, *Mourner's Book of Faith*; Wolfelt, *Loving from the Outside In*.
28. Chatham, "Bereavement Counseling."
29. For helpful booklets on grief, see Wally Stephenson's Grief series; see also Stephenson, *Questions Children and Adults Ask about Grief and Death*.

Chapter 3

1. Randy Lasse, e-mail message to author, January 5, 2018.
2. Doug Amundson, e-mail message to author, January 3, 2018.
3. Randy Lasse, e-mail message to author, January 5, 2018.
4. Samuel Hornbrook, e-mail message to author, January 3, 2018.
5. Samuel Hornbrook, e-mail message to author, January 3, 2018.
6. Kevin Maki, e-mail message to author, January 4, 2018.
7. Roy Jones, e-mail message to author, January 4, 2018. For further descriptions of funerals in Spain, see http://americansevillana.tumblr.com/post/51914681697; http://blog.sevenponds.com/cultural-perspectives/tradition-spanish-funeral.
8. Joshua Stewart, e-mail message to author, January 11, 2018.
9. Ronald Minton, e-mail message to author, January 4, 2018.
10. Kopf, *Canopy of Darkness*, 28–30. The hopelessness of the Hewa tribal group of Papua New Guinea in death is overwhelming.
11. Schaff, *History of the Christians' Church*, 2:74.
12. Schaff, 2:88.
13. Schaff, *History of the Christians' Church*, 3:264.
14. Schaff, 3:819.
15. Carson, *Colonial Experience*, 47.
16. Cairns, *Christianity through the Centuries*, 369.
17. Stannard, *Puritan Way of Life*, 103–4.
18. Stannard, 105, 109.
19. Stannard, 111.
20. Stannard, 116.
21. "Seven Strange Facts about Colonial Funerals," http://www.newenglandhistoricalsociety.com/.
22. "The Dying Ritual," http://www.public.gettysburg.edu/.

23. Linda K. Lewis, "Burial Grounds of Colonial America," http://www.digitalcemetery.glogspot.com/.

Chapter 4

1. Dumond, "Eight Point Eight Two." Another author gives a term as short as three to five years. Lamey, "How Long Should You Stay?"
2. Rainer, "Six Reasons Why Longer-Tenured Pastorates Are Better."
3. Lambert, "Amos Fortune."
4. Lamey, "How Long Should You Stay?"
5. Mitchell and Anderson, *All Our Losses, All Our Griefs*, 54–55.
6. Mitchell and Anderson, 61.
7. Perry and Lias, *A Manual of Pastoral Problems and Procedures*, 148.
8. Adams, *Shepherding God's Flock*, 110–25. Though this volume is more than forty years old, Adams' chapters "Visiting the Sick" and "The Hospital Call" will be invaluable to you if you are new to the pastorate. HIPAA laws will prevent you from discovering the nature and condition of the patient from the medical personnel, as he suggests, but in contrast, people today seem to be much more open to telling the pastor their medical history than they have been in the past.
9. Adams, *Shepherding God's Flock*, 135. Appendix A will give you much material to ponder in light of ministering to the grieving sheep with regard to immediate and long-term care.
10. Unless you are in a culture that demands burial within twenty-four hours, funeral or memorial arrangements can be made after the family has gotten some rest. Depending on the day of the week, out-of-town guests, holidays, and so on, the services will be three to five days away or longer.

Chapter 5

1. "Timeline for Jewish Traditions in Death and Mourning," http://www.econdolence.com/learn/articles/judaism-funeral-burial-customs/, https://www.chabad.org/library/article_cdo/aid/1488006/jewish/Why-the-Rush-for-the-Jewish-Funeral.htm; "Muslim Funeral Traditions," https://www.everplans.com/articles/muslim-funeral-traditions.
2. Rom. 12:15.
3. Thiessen, *Pastoring the Smaller Church*, 138.
4. Many times, these terms are used interchangeably, but as our culture continues to change, I have noted differences. A funeral service is used when the body is present. The memorial service is used when the body is not present. A celebration of life is used when the family wants to focus on the life and accomplishments of the individual rather than his death. "Memorial Services," http://www.aberdeenfuneralhome.com/

memorial-services.
5. "Price List of Pinehill Cemetery in Davenport, IA," http://www.pinehillcemeterydavenport.com/media/DIR_4401/7b2aa0364051e060ffff804effffe904.pdf.
6. 1 Cor. 16:20. A hug even between men at this time is socially acceptable in our culture.
7. 1 Cor. 15:55.
8. *Dictionary.com*, "bereaved," accessed July 25, 2018, http://www.dictionary.com/browse/bereaved.

Chapter 6

1. Gen. 42:21.
2. *Strong's Hebrew Dictionary*, s.v. "tsarah," H6869.
3. Baxter, "Moderate in an Age of Extremes."
4. Blackwood, *The Funeral*, 13.
5. "Top 10 New Funeral Trends," http://www.talkdeath.com/top-new-funeral-trends/.
6. Mark Allen, "10 Trends in 2015 That Were Wake-Up Calls for Funeral Providers," http://goldenruleh.wordpress.com/.
7. John 11.
8. Eph. 5:19–20; Col. 3:16.
9. Goldstein, *Secret Language of the Heart*. Though the book is not a religious or spiritual text, the reader will gain insight on the healing and transformational nature of music.
10. Fettke, *Celebration Hymnal*, hymn 776.
11. Wyrtzen, "Finally Home."
12. 1 Tim. 4:13.
13. Neh. 8:8; Jer. 36:8, 51:63; Acts 13:15; 2 Cor. 3:14; 1 Tim. 4:13.
14. Thiessen, *Pastoring the Smaller Church*, 139.
15. Thiessen.
16. For more instructions, see Toastmasters, "Creating Powerful Introductions and Conclusions," https://www.toastmasters.org/Magazine/Articles/For-the-Novice-From-Hello-to-Goodbye.
17. Perry and Lias, *A Manual of Pastoral Problems and Procedures*, 128.
18. 1 Thes. 4:13.
19. Eph. 2:12.
20. 1 Cor. 15:3–4; Rom. 4:25. One of the driving forces of this book is that I have attended too many funerals where "the Gospel" was mentioned and never defined, or I never heard one word regarding the death, burial, and resurrection of Christ, or it was lost in dead ritual. Do not tack it on at the end. Make the Gospel the foundational truth of your ministry to

the sorrowing; otherwise, we are no better than the false witnesses (1 Cor. 15:15).
21. Hermiz and Tolen, *Pastor's Funeral Planner*, 22.
22. The International Conference of Police Chaplains has a helpful website and manuals published where you can find help and the name of a police chaplain to learn the accepted protocol for officer funerals: http://www.icpc4cops.org/.
23. Titus 2:13.

Chapter 7

1. McClendon, *Doctrine: Systematic Theology*, 2:84.
2. 1 Cor. 15:54–57.
3. 2 Cor. 5:6–8.
4. 2 Thes. 1:8–9; 2 Pet. 2:9.
5. Barnes, *Barnes' Notes*, 235.
6. Matt. 25:34–36; Phil. 3:9; Rev. 20:5–6.
7. Barnes, *Barnes' Notes*, 235; Matt. 25:46; Rev. 20:12–15.
8. You have noted that I use three terms regarding this service: *graveside*, *interment (inurnment)*, and *committal*. They can be defined as follows: a graveside service is a funeral service held at the gravesite at a cemetery. A graveside service can follow a traditional funeral or can be a stand-alone event. It is a type of service that can be held for either burial or interment of cremated remains. https://www.everplans.com/articles/how-to-plan-a-graveside-service. Interment (or inurnment in the case of cremation) is referring to the act of burial. Committal refers to the ritual associated with the burial.
9. *Ohio Revised Code*, "Right of Way of Funeral Vehicle," http://codes.ohio.gov/orc/4511.451.
10. Perry and Lias, *A Manual of Pastoral Problems and Procedures*, 129. See also Thiessen, *Pastoring the Smaller Church*, 140.
11. The authors, Perry and Lias, recommend in their book *A Manual of Pastoral Problems and Procedures* the following volumes: Wm. H. Leach, *The Improved Funeral Manual* (Grand Rapids, Mich.: Baker Book House, 1956); Robert G. Seymour, *Pastor's Companion for Weddings and Funerals* (Philadelphia: Judson Press, 1898); Edward T. Hiscox, *The Star Book for Ministers* (Philadelphia: Hudson Press, 1951).
12. Rom. 16:16; 1 Cor. 16:20; 2 Cor. 13:12; 1 Thess. 5:26.
13. "Funerals," http://www.wingsaway.info/.
14. Furman, *How to Plan a Funeral*, 68.
15. Michael Peck, e-mail message to author, January 4, 2018.

Chapter 8
1. https://www.cdc.gov/nchs/fastats/deaths.htm.
2. https://www.bls.gov/ooh/personal-care-and-services/mobile/funeral-service-occupations.htm.
3. National Funeral Directors Association, http://www.nfda.org/.
4. Bureau of Labor Statistics, *Occupational Outlook Handbook*, 1066.
5. Carlson, *Caring for the Dead*, 43–45. Also "Home Funerals: Caring for Our Own Dead," http://www.fcaofmn.org/home-funerals-caring-for-our-own-dead.html.
6. Bureau of Labor Statistics, *Occupational Outlook Handbook*, 1066–69; Ferguson, "Funeral Home Workers."
7. National Funeral Directors' Association, http://www.nfda.org/news/statistics.
8. SurveyMonkey results ranged from sixty-five annually to twelve hundred company-wide, i.e., multiple chapels. *Funeral Directors and Pastors*, April 2018.
9. National Funeral Directors' Association, http://www.nfda.org/news/statistics; Institute for Career Research, *Career as a Funeral Director, Mortuary Science, Embalmer*.
10. SurveyMonkey results, *Funeral Directors and Pastors*, April 2018.
11. SurveyMonkey results.
12. SurveyMonkey results.
13. SurveyMonkey results.
14. SurveyMonkey results.
15. Long and Linch, *The Good Funeral*, 157–58.
16. Carlson, *Caring for the Dead*, 609–12.

Chapter 9
1. Romm, "Why Comfort Food Comforts."
2. *Strong's Concordance*, s.v. "comfort."
3. "Funeral Food," https://www.funeralwise.com/plan/celebration-of-life/funeral-food/.
4. Beal, "How to Plan a Funeral Luncheon."
5. A very helpful website for determining amounts is https://www.chef-menus.com/food-quantity-chart.html.
6. Furman, *How to Plan a Funeral*, 32–33.

Chapter 10
1. Survey Monkey Results, *Funerals and Memorial Services* (San Mateo, Calif.: SurveyMonkey, April 2018), http://www.surveymonkey.com/.
2. James 3:10.

3. Thiessen, *Pastoring the Smaller Church*, 140–41; Perry and Lias, *A Manual of Pastoral Problems and Procedures*, 129.
4. Hermiz and Toler, *Pastor's Funeral Planner*, 149–51.
5. Hybels, *Just Walk across the Room*, 60.
6. Wagner, *The Pastor*, 309.
7. Sanders, *Law Enforcement Funeral Manual*, 61.
8. Furman, *How to Plan a Funeral*, 79.
9. Furman.
10. *Strong's Concordance*, s.v. "need."
11. "The Dying Ritual," http://public.gettysburg.edu/~tshannon/341/sites/Death%20and%20Mourning/dying_ritual.htm.
12. Bailey, *Biblical Perspectives on Death*, 108.
13. Bailey, 107.
14. Kilner et al., *Dignity and Dying*, 238.
15. Mitchell and Anderson, *All Our Losses*, 111.
16. Adams, *Shepherding God's Flock*, 155–56.
17. Laurie A. Erickson, lecture given at the Michigan State Police Academy, October 8, 1999, quoted by Sanders, *Law Enforcement Funeral Manual*, 62.
18. Perry and Lias, *A Manual of Pastoral Problems and Procedure*, 129.
19. Kuenning, *Helping People through Grief*, 256–59.
20. Schaeffer, *Affliction*, 169–89.

Chapter 11

1. The following is a summary of the SurveyMonkey answers from fifty-five pastors to the question "What advice would you give to an inexperienced pastor on how to perform a funeral?" April 2018.
2. James 3:13–18.
3. Hiscox, *Star Book for Ministers*, 34–41. Two revisions have followed: 1906 and 1994.
4. Thiessen, *Pastoring the Smaller Church*, 137.
5. SurveyMonkey Response, *Pastors and Funerals*, April 2018.
6. Wagner, *The Pastor*, 306.
7. Wagner, 307.
8. SurveyMonkey results, *Funerals and Memorial Services*, April 2018.
9. Thiessen, *Pastoring the Smaller Church*, 139.
10. Chapell, *Christ-Centered Preaching*, 344.
11. Chapell, 346.
12. SurveyMonkey results, *Pastors and Funerals*, April 2018.
13. SurveyMonkey results, *Pastors and Funerals*, April 2018.
14. Thiessen, *Pastoring the Smaller Church*, 140.
15. Wagner, *The Pastor*, 310–11.

16. Sanders, *Law Enforcement Funeral Manual*; American Legion, *American Legion Officer's Guide and Manual of Ceremonies*.

Epilogue

1. From chapter 1. Quote is from Berkhof, *Systematic Theology*, 261.
2. From chapter 2. See also Woodard, *Ministry of Presence*.
3. From chapter 1.
4. From chapter 3. See also Kopf, *Canopy of Darkness*, 28-30. The hopelessness of the Hewa tribal group of Papua New Guinea in death is overwhelming.
5. From chapter 4. Quote is from Mitchell and Anderson, *All Our Losses*, 54-55.
6. 1 Cor. 15:12-22.
7. From chapter 1.
8. From chapter 1 and Ryrie, *A Survey of Bible Doctrine*, 62-64. See Cairns, *Christianity through the Centuries*, 481.
9. From chapter 1.
10. From chapter 10.
11. From chapter 11.

Resources

1. Thiessen, *Pastoring the Smaller Church*, 139.
2. Service order for Leslie Newell, retired missionary, December 23, 2017.
3. Service order for James Dennis, retired pastor, January 13, 2018.
4. Perry and Lias, *Pastoral Problems and Procedures*, 128.
5. Spencer, *Hymn and Scripture Selection Guide*, 85, 185, 213, 233, 265-66, 276, 303.
6. Multiple pastors surveyed indicated this as one of their favorite passages.
7. Wernecke, *When Love Ones Are Called Home*, 73-74.
8. SurveyMonkey results, *Pastors and Funerals*, April 2018.
9. These are sermon outlines I have used at funerals. They will get you started, but make them your own!
10. Henry Morris III, *Days of Praise* (Dallas: Institute of Creation Research, 2018).
11. Michael Peck, e-mail message to author, July 3, 2018.
12. Peck.
13. Peck.
14. Sanders, *Law Enforcement Funeral Manual*, 66.
15. Wright, *Journey in Grief Care*.

BIBLIOGRAPHY

Adams, Jay E. *Christ and Your Problems*. Phillipsburg, N.J.: P and R, 1971.
———. *The Christian Counselor's Manual*. Grand Rapids, Mich.: Baker Book House, 1973.
———. *Shepherding God's Flock: A Handbook on Pastoral Ministry, Counseling and Leadership*. Grand Rapids, Mich.: Zondervan, 1974.
Allen, Mark. "10 Trends in 2015 That Were Wake-Up Calls for Funeral Providers." *Order of the Golden Rule* (blog), January 5, 2016. http://blog.ogr.org/.
American Legion. *American Legion Officer's Guide and Manual of Ceremonies*. Indianapolis, Ind.: American Legion National Headquarters, 2013.
Bailey, Lloyd R., Sr. *Biblical Perspectives on Death*. Philadelphia: Fortress Press, 1979.
Bancroft, Emery H. *Elemental Theology*. Grand Rapids, Mich.: Kregel, 1977.
Barnes, Albert. *Barnes' Notes: Notes on the New Testament–Luke and John*. Grand Rapids, Mich.: Baker Books, 1996.
Bauman, Harold. *Grief's Slow Work*. Scottdale, Pa.: Herald Press, 1960.
Baxter, Richard. "Moderate in an Age of Extremes." *Christianity Today*. http://www.chritianitytoday.com/history/people/pastorsandpreachers/richard-baxter.html.
Beal, Janet. "How to Plan a Funeral Luncheon." *Our Everyday Life* (blog), September 29, 2017. https://oureverydaylife.com/how-to-plan-a-funeral-luncheon-12078956.html.
Bennett, Ivan L., ed. *Song and Service Book for Ship and Field: Army and Navy*. New York: A. S. Barnes, 1941.
Berkhof, Louis. *Systematic Theology*. Grand Rapids, Mich.: Wm. B. Eerdmans, 1939.
Biddle, Perry H. *A Funeral Manual*. Grand Rapids, Mich.: Wm. B. Eerdmans, 1994.
Blackwood, Andrew W. *The Funeral: A Source Book for Ministers*. Philadelphia: Westminster Press, 1942.

Bonner, William J. *In Time of Sorrow: A Funeral Manual.* Grand Rapids, Mich.: Zondervan, 1942.

Bridges, Jerry. *Trusting God.* Colorado Springs, Colo.: NavPress, 1988.

Brown, Francis, C. Briggs, and S. R. Driver. *The Brown–Driver–Briggs Hebrew and English Lexicon.* Peabody, Mass.: Hendrickson, 1996.

Bunyan, John. *The Pilgrim's Progress.* New Kensington, Pa.: Whitaker House, 1973.

Bureau of Labor Statistics. "Funeral Service Workers." https://www.bls.gov/ooh/personal-care-and-services/mobile/funeral-service-occupations.htm.

Bureau of Labor Statistics. *Occupational Outlook Handbook: 2014–2015 Edition.* Baton Rouge, La.: Claitor's, 2014.

Byers, Dale A. *Suicide: How God Sustained a Family.* Schaumburg, Ill.: Regular Baptist Press, 1991.

Byrum, Russell R. *Christian Theology.* Anderson, Ind.: Warner Press, 1925.

Cadenhead, Al, Jr. *The Minister's Manual for Funerals.* Nashville, Tenn.: Broadman and Holman, 1988.

Cairns, Earle E. *Christianity through the Centuries.* Grand Rapids, Mich.: Zondervan, 1954.

Carlson, Lisa. *Caring for the Dead: Your Final Act of Love.* Hinesburg, Vt.: Upper Access Books, 1988.

Carlson, Neal. *To Die Is Gain.* Grand Rapids, Mich.: Baker Book House, 1974.

Carson, Clarence. *The Colonial Experience: 1607–1774.* Wadley, Ga.: American Textbook Committee, 1983.

Carson, D. A. *How Long, O Lord? Reflections on Suffering and Evil.* Grand Rapids, Mich.: Baker Academic, 2006.

Chafer, Lewis Sperry. *Systematic Theology.* Grand Rapids, Mich.: Kregel, 1993.

Chapell, Bryan. *Christ-Centered Preaching.* Grand Rapids, Mich.: Baker Book House, 1994.

Chatham, James. "Bereavement Counseling." Class lecture, Trinity Theological Seminary, Newburgh, Ind., April 19, 2015.

Cherry, Constance M. *The Special Service Worship Architect.* Grand Rapids, Mich.: Baker Academic, 2013.

Christensen, James L. *The Compete Funeral Manual.* Old Tappan, N.J.: Fleming H. Revell, 1967.

———. *Funeral Services for Today.* Old Tappan, N.J.: Fleming H. Revell, 1977.

Clarke, Adam. *Adam Clarke's Commentary on the Bible.* Bellingham, Wash.: Faithlife Corporation, 2014.

Couch, Mal, ed. *The Fundamentals for the Twenty-First Century.* Grand Rapids, Mich.: Kregel, 2000.

Curtis, Olin A. *The Christian Faith.* New York: Eaton and Mains, 1905.

Davis, Ron Lee. *Gold in the Making: Where Is God When Bad Things Happen to You?* Nashville, Tenn.: Thomas Nelson, 1983.

Dumond, Franklin. "Eight Point Eight Two: How Long Do Pastors Stay in One Church?" *General Baptist News*, June 26, 2014. http://www.gbjournal.org/.

Elliot, Elbert E. "Theology of Ministry." Class lecture, Trinity Theological Seminary, Newburgh, Ind., August, 14, 2012.

Engle, Paul E. *Baker's Funeral Handbook*. Grand Rapids, Mich.: Baker Books, 1996.

Evans, William. *The Great Doctrines of the Bible*. Chicago: Bible Institute Colportage Association, 1912.

Ferguson. "Funeral Home Workers." In *Encyclopedia of Careers and Vocational Guidance*, 14th ed., Article D-1. New York: Ferguson, 2005.

Fettke, Tom. *The Celebration Hymnal: Songs and Hymns for Worship*. Brentwood, Tenn.: Word Music/Integrity Music, 1997.

Fitzgerald, Helen. *The Mourning Handbook*. New York: Fireside, 1994.

Furman, Liz Cowen. *How to Plan a Funeral*. Kansas City, Mo.: Beacon Hill Press, 2008.

Geisler, Norman. *Systematic Theology*. Vol. 3. Minneapolis, Minn.: Bethany House, 2004.

Goldstein, Barry. *The Secret Language of the Heart*. San Antonio, Tex.: Hierophant, 2016.

Gorman, Cinda. "When a Child Dies." *Leadership*, Winter 1998.

Harris, Mark. *A Journey through a Modern Funeral*. New York: Scribner, 2007.

Harris, Trudy. *Glimpses of Heaven*. Grand Rapids, Mich.: Revell, 2008.

Harrison, Norman B. *His Comfort: A Message of Help for Those Who Sorrow*. Minneapolis, Minn.: Harrison Service, 1937.

Henry, Matthew. *Matthew Henry's Commentary on the Whole Bible*. Peabody, Mass.: Hendrickson, 2014.

Hermiz, Thomas H., and Stan Toler. *The Pastor's Funeral Planner*. Kansas City, Mo.: Beacon Hill Press, 2011.

Hiscox, Edward. *The Star Book for Ministers*. 3rd rev ed. Valley Forge, Pa.: Judson Press. Originally published 1878.

Hodge, Charles. *Systematic Theology*. Vol. 2. Grand Rapids, Mich.: Wm. B. Eerdmans, 1970.

Horton, Michael. *The Christian Faith*. Grand Rapids, Mich.: Zondervan, 2011.

Hybels, Bill. *Just Walk across the Room*. Grand Rapids, Mich.: Zondervan, 2006.

Institute for Career Research. *Career as a Funeral Director, Mortuary Science, Embalmer*. Chicago: Institute for Career Research, 2018.

Jamison, Robert, A. R. Fausset, and David Brown. *Commentary Critical and Explanatory on the Whole Bible.* 1871. https://www.biblestudytools.com/commentaries/jamieson-fausset-brown/.
Josephson, Amelia. "How Much Does the Average Funeral Cost?" March 2, 2016. https://smartasset.com/life-insurance/how-much-does-the-average-funeral-cost.
Keil, C. F., and F. Delitzsch. *Biblical Commentary on the Old Testament.* Vol. 1. Grand Rapids, Mich.: Wm. B. Eerdmans, 1959.
Kilner, John F., Arlene B. Miller, and Edward D. Pellegrino. *Dignity and Dying: A Christian Appraisal.* Grand Rapids, Mich.: Wm. B. Eerdmans, 1996.
Kopf, Jonathan. *Canopy of Darkness.* Dallas, Tex.: Entrust Source, 2013.
Kubler-Ross, Elizabeth. *On Death and Dying.* New York: Scribner, 1969.
Kuenning, Delores. *Helping People through Grief.* Minneapolis, Minn.: Bethany House, 1987.
Kushner, Harold S. *When Bad Things Happen to Good People.* New York: Avon Books, 1981.
Lambert, Peter. *Amos Fortune: The Man and His Legacy.* Brochure.
Lamey, Paul. "How Long Should You Stay at Your Church?" October 8, 2015. http://www.expositors.org/blog/how-long-should-you-stay-at-your-church/
Leach, William H. *The Improved Funeral Manual.* Grand Rapids, Mich.: Baker Book House, 1956.
Leupold, H. C. *Exposition of Genesis.* Vol. 2. Grand Rapids, Mich.: Baker Book House, 1942.
Lewis, Clive Staples. *A Grief Observed.* New York: HarperCollins, 1961.
Lewis, Linda K. "Burial Grounds of Colonial America." *The Digital Cemetery* (blog), October 5, 2007. http://www.digitalcemetery.blogspot.com/.
Lewis, Tayler, and A. Gosman, A. *Lange's Commentary on the Holy Scriptures,* vol. 1, *Genesis.* Grand Rapids, Mich.: Zondervan, 1971.
Lloyd, Dan S. *Leading Today's Funerals.* Grand Rapids, Mich.: Baker Books, 1997.
Lloyd-Jones, D. M. *The Puritans: Their Origins and Successors.* Carlisle, Pa.: Banner of Truth Trust, 1987.
Lockyer, Herbert. *All the Parables of the Bible.* Grand Rapids, Mich.: Zondervan, 1963.
———. *The Funeral Sourcebook.* Grand Rapids, Mich.: Zondervan, 1967.
Long, Thomas G., and Thomas Linch. *The Good Funeral: Death, Grief, and the Community of Care.* Louisville, Ky.: Westminster John Knox Press, 2013.
Mackintosh, C. H. *Notes on the Book of Genesis.* Neptune, N.J.: Loizeaux Brothers, 1965.

Macquarrie, John. *Principles of Christian Theology.* New York: Charles Scribner's Sons, 1966.
Malphurs, Aubrey, and Keith Willhite, eds. *A Contemporary Handbook for Weddings and Funerals.* Grand Rapids, Mich.: Kregel, 2003.
Manning, Doug. *The Funeral: A Chance to Touch, a Chance to Serve, a Chance to Heal.* Oklahoma City, Okla.: In-Sight Books, 2001.
———. *The Power of Presence: Helping People Help People.* Oklahoma City, Okla.: In-Sight Books, 2013.
Mansell, John S. *The Funeral: A Pastor's Guide.* Nashville, Tenn.: Abingdon Press, 1998.
Marks, Amy S., and Bobby J. Calder. *Attitudes toward Death and Funerals.* Evanston, Ill.: Center for Marketing Sciences, J. L. Kellogg Graduate School of Management, Northwestern University, 1982.
McClendon, James W., Jr. *Doctrine: Systematic Theology.* Vol. 2. Nashville, Tenn.: Abingdon Press, 1994.
M'Cheyne, Robert M. *Comfort in Sickness and Death.* Grand Rapids, Mich.: Baker Book House, 1976.
Mitchell, Kenneth R., and Herbert Anderson. *All Our Losses, All Our Griefs: Resources for Pastoral Care.* Philadelphia: Westminster Press, 1983.
Morgan, John D., and Pittu Laungani, ed. *Death and Bereavement around the World.* Amityville, N.Y.: Baywood, 2002.
Motter, Alton M., ed. *Preaching about Death.* Philadelphia: Fortress Press, 1975.
Murphy, James G. *Barnes' Notes: A Commentary on the Book of Genesis.* Grand Rapids, Mich.: Baker Book House, 1966.
Oates, Wayne. *Grief, Transition, and Loss: A Pastor's Practical Guide.* Minneapolis: Fortress Press, 1997.
Oyedele, Akin. "It's Gotten a Whole Lot More Expensive to Die in America." *Business Insider*, October 31, 2017. http://www.businessinsider.com/.
Palmer, Judson B. *The Child of God: Between Death and the Resurrection.* Minneapolis, Minn.: Osterhus, 1946.
Perry, Lloyd M., and Edward J. Lias. *A Manual of Pastoral Problems and Procedures.* Grand Rapids, Mich.: Baker Book House, 1962.
Pfeiffer, Charles F. *The Book of Genesis: A Study Manual.* Grand Rapids, Mich.: Baker Book House, 1958.
Pine, Vanderlyn R. *Caretaker of the Dead: The American Funeral Director.* New York: Iverington, 1975.
Power, Paul W. *Why Me Lord?* Wheaton, Ill.: Victor Books, 1981.
Price, Eugenia. *Getting through the Night.* New York: Dial Press, 1982.
Price, Roy. "Building Trust between Pastor and Congregation." *Christianity Today*, Spring 1980. http://www.christianitytoday.com/.

Purkiser, Westlake T. *Exploring Our Christian Faith*. Kansas City, Mo.: Beacon Hill Press, 1960.

Rainer, Thomas S. "Six Reasons Why Longer-Tenured Pastorates Are Better." *Thom Rainer* (blog), November 16, 2015. http://www.thomrainer.com/.

Rice, John R. *Bible Facts about Heaven: Sweet Home of Departed Saints*. Murfreesboro, Tenn.: Sword of the Lord, 1940.

Romm, Cari. "Why Comfort Food Comforts." *Atlantic*, April 3, 2015. https://www.theatlantic.com/health/archive/2015/04/why-comfort-food-comforts/389613/.

Ryrie, Charles C. *A Survey of Bible Doctrine*. Chicago: Moody, 1972.

———. *Basic Theology*. Wheaton, Ill.: Victor Books, 1986.

Sanders, Catherine. *Grief: The Mourning After*. Hoboken, N.J.: John Wiley, 1999.

Sanders, William P. *Law Enforcement Funeral Manual*. Springfield, Ill.: Charles C. Thomas, 2006.

Saxman, James. "Ministering to Those Who Mourn." *Baptist Bulletin*, March/April 2017.

Schaeffer, Edith. *Affliction*. Old Tappan, N.J.: Fleming H. Reveal, 1978.

Schaff, Philip. *History of the Christians' Church*, vol. 7, *The German Reformation*. Grand Rapids, Mich.: Wm. B. Eerdmans, 1910.

———. *History of the Christians' Church*, vol. 8, *The Swiss Reformation*. Grand Rapids, Mich.: Wm. B. Eerdmans, 1910.

———. *Lange's Commentary on the Holy Scriptures*, vol. 8, *Luke*. Grand Rapids, Mich.: Zondervan, 1971.

Seymour, Robert G. *Pastor's Companion for Weddings and Funerals*. Philadelphia: Judson Press, 1898.

Smith, Harold Ivan. *When You Don't Know What To Say: How to Help Your Grieving Friends*. Kansas City, Mo.: Beacon Hill Press, 2002.

Spencer, Donald A. *Hymn and Scripture Selection Guide*. Grand Rapids, Mich.: Baker Book House, 1993.

Stafford, Tim. *As Our Years Increase: Loving, Caring, Preparing: A Guide*. Grand Rapids, Mich.: Zondervan, 1989.

Stannard, David E. *The Puritan Way of Life*. New York: Oxford University Press, 1977.

Stephenson, Wally. *Helping a Friend Who Is Grieving*. Harrisburg, Pa.: ABWE.

———. *Helping Friends and Family of an Unbeliever Who Dies*. Harrisburg, Pa.: ABWE.

———. *Ministering Help and Hope to the Dying*. Harrisburg, Pa.: ABWE.

———. *Questions Children and Adults Ask about Grief and Death*. Schaumburg, Ill.: Regular Baptist Press, 2003.

———. *What Grievers Can Expect*. Harrisburg, Pa.: ABWE.

Strauss, Lehman. *When Loved Ones Are Taken in Death*. Fincastle, Va.: Scripture Truth, n.d.

Strong, A. H. *Systematic Theology*. Vol. 2. Philadelphia: Griffith and Rowland Press, 1907.

Strong, James. *Strong's Expanded Exhaustive Concordance of the Bible*. Iowa Falls: Riverside Book and Bible House, n.d.

Thiessen, Henry C. *Introductory Lectures in Systematic Theology*. Grand Rapids, Mich.: Wm. B. Eerdmans, 1949.

Thiessen, John C. *Pastoring the Smaller Church*. Grand Rapids, Mich.: Zondervan, 1962.

Wagner, Charles U. *The Pastor: His Life and Work*. Schaumburg, Ill.: Regular Baptist Press, 1976.

Wallis, Charles L., ed. *The Funeral Encyclopedia: A Source Book*. New York: Harper, 1953.

Walvoord, John F., and Roy B. Zuck. *The Bible Knowledge Commentary: New Testament Edition*. Wheaton, Ill.: Victor Books, 1989.

———. *The Bible Knowledge Commentary: Old Testament*. Wheaton, Ill.: Victor Books, 1989.

Wernecke, Herbert. *When Loved Ones Are Called Home*. Grand Rapids, Mich.: Baker Book House, 1950.

Wiersbe, Warren W. *Be Courageous*. Colorado Springs, Colo.: Chariot Victor, 1989.

———. *Looking Up When Life Gets You Down*. Grand Rapids, Mich.: Baker Books, 2012.

Willimon, William, Dallas Willard, Larry Burkett et al. *The Pastor's Guide to Effective Ministry*. Kansas City, Mo.: Beacon Hill Press, 2002.

Winokuer, Howard R., and Darcy L. Harris. *Principles and Practice of Grief Counseling*. New York: Springer, 2012.

Wolfelt, Alan. *The Handbook for Companioning the Mourner*. Fort Collins, Colo.: Companion Press, 2009.

———. "Helping Homicide Survivors Heal." *Frontline*, Spring 2017.

———. *Loving from the Outside In, Mourning from the Inside Out*. Fort Collins, Colo.: Companion Press, 2012.

———. *The Mourner's Book of Faith*. Fort Collins, Colo.: Companion Press, 2013.

———. *Understanding Your Grief*. Fort Collins, Colo.: Companion Press, 2003.

Woodard, Whit. *Ministry of Presence*. North Fort Myers, Fla.: Faithful Life, 2011.

Worden, J. William. *Grief Counseling and Grief Therapy*. New York: Springer, 2009.

Wright, H. Norman. *Helping Those in Grief: A Guide to Help You Care for Others.* Bloomington, Minn.: Bethany House, 2011.

Wyrtzen, Don. "Finally Home." In *Going Home (75 Songs for Funerals, Memorial Services and Life Celebrations).* Chicago: Brentwood-Benson, n.d.

www.ingramcontent.com/pod-product-compliance
Lightning Source LLC
LaVergne TN
LVHW051834080426
835512LV00018B/2880